Additional Praise for *Incline Your Ear*

"Spiritual wisdom never dies. It resides in hearts like those of Chad R. Abbott and Teresa Blythe. *Incline Your Ear,* their gift to us all, opens a pathway to spirit-filled mission and life. We are all wise to join them on the journey."
—The Rev. Dr. John C. Dorhauer, General Minister and President of the United Church of Christ, author of *Beyond Resistance: The Institutional Church Meets the Postmodern World*

"Chad R. Abbott and Teresa Blythe have written the book I wish had been available when I was a pastor. They have intertwined their wisdom into a seamless narrative, supporting us as we travel together on a congregational spiritual road trip. *Incline Your Ear* is a congregational pilgrimage that focuses our intention on the vital work of deep listening and intentional discernment. Abbott and Blythe have written a rare book. *Incline Your Ear* is filled with the practical resources and tools necessary to develop a discerning community—a congregation that will turn toward God with the ear of a unified heart."
—The Rev. Gil Stafford, author of *When Leadership and Spiritual Direction Meet: Stories and Reflections for Congregational Life* and *Wisdom Walking: Pilgrimage as a Way of Life*

"*Incline Your Ear* is an excellent resource to help congregations grow in listening to and discerning God's direction. They offer a variety of tools, all clearly accessible for both beginners and those more experienced in spiritual practices. Theologically and

biblically grounded, it will bear fruit in many faith traditions."
—The Rev. Victoria Curtiss, spiritual director, pastor, and author of *Guidelines for Communal Discernment*

"*Incline Your Ear* provides a holistic vision of personal and congregational transformation, reminding congregations and their leaders that the process of spiritual discernment is their most effective tool for decision-making. In a time in which many see the congregation as the last place to nurture spiritual growth, *Incline Your Ear* asserts that every aspect of congregational life can deepen our spirituality. Written by two experienced pastors and spiritual guides, this text is profoundly incarnational. God is present in our daily lives, professional activities, and vocations and avocations. God is equally present when congregations make decisions regarding budgets, personnel, mission, and the challenges of institutional survival. Chad R. Abbott and Teresa Blythe remind us that we are always on holy ground and that caring for brick and mortar, managing finances, and planning are spiritual activities in which we can find both personal meaning and congregational vocation. I was inspired as I read this text. It provides a wealth of insights and practices for congregational leadership in this time of protest and pandemic. I highly recommend *Incline Your Ear* for any leader or congregational community who is seeking spiritual guidance in facing the uncertainties and challenges of the twenty-first century."
—The Rev. Dr. Bruce Epperly, pastor at the South Congregational Church, United Church of Christ, and the author of *A Center in the Cyclone: Twenty-First Century Clergy Self-Care* and *Tending to the Holy: The Practice the Presence of God in Ministry*

"Living as we do in a world so noisy that it drives us to distraction, Chad R. Abbott and Teresa Blythe have correctly identified the core issue. As individual Christians, and together as the

church, we need to 'incline our ear' toward the God who would bring us and the world to healing and renewal. Currently, a primary weakness in the body of Christ is a lack of spiritual formation that equips the people to hear, reflect, discern, and respond. This book provides the direction and needed resources to shape the journey toward spiritual health and effective mission."
—The Rev. Dr. Dick Hamm, former General and Minister and President of the Christian Church (Disciples of Christ)

"*Incline Your Ear* is abundantly rich in all that it gently and brilliantly offers to congregations and to those of us who love and serve congregations and are committed to the way of Christ. It is a book rich in Scripture; in Christian traditions; in practical, approachable prayer practices; and in effective ways to engage in the deep work of discernment that can lead toward action. We can trust this road map to help us expand our trust in the Spirit and in ourselves."
—The Rev. Kim Gage Ryan, codirector and pastor of Bethany Fellows

# Incline Your Ear

# Incline Your Ear

Cultivating Spiritual Awakening in
Congregations

Chad R. Abbott and Teresa Blythe

Foreword by J. Brent Bill

**Fortress Press**

Minneapolis

INCLINE YOUR EAR

Cultivating Spiritual Awakening in Congregations

Scripture quotations are from the New Revised Standard Version Bible © 1989 Division of Christian Education of the National Council of the Churches of Christ in the United States of America. Used by permission.

Cover designer: Laurie Ingram

Cover image: Inside of Nautilus Shell/Design Pics/Superstock

Print ISBN: 978-1-5064-6583-8

Ebook ISBN: 978-1-5064-6584-5

# Contents

# Foreword

The church is too busy, often with church business instead of the true business of the church. We rush to committees, commissions, meetings, and more. We often return to our homes after such gatherings discouraged or burned out, our souls hungry for spiritual food.

The Quaker mystic Thomas Kelly wrote, "We are pulled and hauled breathlessly along by an over-burdened program of good committees and good undertakings. I am persuaded that this fevered life of church workers is not wholesome."[1]

Indeed, it is not. It's not, because the fevered life of church workers on these good committees and undertakings is not the true business of the church. The true business of the church is developing the spiritual life of its members individually and collectively.

The small Quaker congregation I belong to learned that lesson a decade ago. While wrestling with finding enough people to serve on the committees and positions that were outlined in our book of discipline, people were feeling overburdened and overwhelmed. A sense of despair about our future was settling upon us.

Then Ministry and Counsel (the Quaker version of a spiritual life/worship committee) came to the membership with a recommendation that we lay down (Quakerese for abolish) all committees except Ministry and Counsel.

The minutes of that meeting for business record that when the recommendation was read, there was an audible gasp from the gathered members. It was also recorded that the gasp was almost immediately followed by a louder sigh of relief.

That action, along with some others recommended by Ministry and Counsel, moved the congregation to a place where we could concentrate on renewing our individual spiritual lives and our collective life together.

Now I wish I could report, for those who think that increased attendance is the mark of congregational success, that our attendance has doubled since we made that decision. It hasn't. But our spiritual lives are deeper and richer. We have focused on things that feed our souls and take us deeper into our life together. And that has attracted new folks, who have joined us as some of our older members have moved on to the life eternal.

Yes, we still conduct business—via short-term working groups that people volunteer to work on as they feel led by God's spirit, not because someone from a nominating committee called them and asked them to fill a vacant three-year term that could be extended for three more years. We as a congregation are learning that our real business is developing an awareness of God around us and in us and through us, in our daily lives and in our times together.

For too long, too many of us who attend worship or committee meetings have left exactly as we came in. Unchanged. Unmoved. We now see that our congregation, having placed its emphasis on developing our spiritual lives, has not left us unchanged, even when that change is not comfortable. Becoming more aware of God in the daily has made us more aware of our need to be active in the causes that are near to the heart of God as we understand it. So, we are in many ways busier than we were before—just not with committee meetings and the like. We are busy in the service of the Eternal, a service that further enriches our souls.

All that I've written above is why this book, *Incline Your Ear: Cultivating Spiritual Awakening in Congregations*, by my friends Chad Abbott and Teresa Blythe is so needed. People around us are hungry for purpose and meaning and spiritual connection. They are not very concerned with maintaining institutions—even those with "good committees and good undertakings." This worthy book will help congregations of all sizes and denominations recover a sense of the true spiritual nature of their mission in this world. We hold a precious gift and invitation. The gift is an awareness of the abundant life Jesus said he came to bring us. The invitation we can offer, our congregations' focus on the call to deepen peoples' lives, is for others to come to experience that abundant life, which grows richer every day. As Chad and Teresa write:

We believe constant awakening is an invitation to learn to be the church, even as the way we express and define ourselves as church continues to emerge and grow. Embrace the journey. Listen deeply. Remain open to the transforming power of God's Spirit in your midst. Incline your ear, for the God who is still speaking awakens us to a new day.

Indeed. And amen.

—J. Brent Bill, Ploughshares Farm

# Preface

It's a familiar scene in churches today. The pastor is on the razor's edge of burnout, trying to be everything to everyone. The moderator of the church board is worried that the church isn't growing because it doesn't have the right "vision." Members say they enjoy church well enough, but frankly they experience more spirituality on their yoga mat. Why aren't our churches meeting the spiritual need that is palpable in our society today?

This question haunts many Christians, and the answers are not very comforting. We live in an increasingly secular world, so spiritual seekers today simply do not think of churches as holy places anymore. Unfortunately, many of the battles Christians engage in with each other reinforce that image. When we make doctrinal litmus tests that people have to pass in order to come and pray with us, we create more blocks than openings in our churches.

And just like the church member who whispers that she gets more spirituality out of yoga than church, some spiritual seekers are experiencing the holy in venues other than churches. That doesn't mean Christians are being kicked to the curb or that we have to start offering yoga instead of Bible study in order to be relevant (although this is not a criticism of churches that host yoga classes). The church still has a lot to offer spiritual seekers. The primary challenge we face is that many of our churches lost their way somewhere along the line and either gave up on prayer and spirituality (which we used to call devotion or discipleship) or managed to emphasize only one kind of prayer, usually a prayer of recitation or petition, leaving out in the cold those who experience God in silence, in physical activity such as walking or body prayer, or through art.

Although it pains us to admit it, some churches drive spiritual seekers away. If our church is unhealthy, rife with conflict and drama, then healthy spiritual seekers will run the other way. If our church demands that a newcomer look, act, and believe the same as everyone already there, spiritual seekers will find a place that accepts them as they are. Churches that are open to exploring spirituality with someone who may be new to Christianity are gentle, nonjudgmental, and humble. If a seeker doesn't find that atmosphere at your church, he or she will look elsewhere.

Another factor that keeps churches from being the spiritual centers they want to be is clergy and leadership burnout. Somewhere along the way, churchgoers adopted the idea that certain jobs in the community are too difficult for just anyone. Thus, these jobs were "outsourced" to the pastor. These jobs usually include visiting people in hospitals or at home, praying with someone (or just praying out loud anywhere), sharing stories of faith, and leading Bible study. What is worse, somewhere along the way, pastors acquiesced. Perhaps it was a need to be needed or the feeling that "if I don't do it, no one will," but this shift has deadening consequences. No pastor can do it all, nor should they even try. This leaves us with a clarifying reality: people in congregations need to understand that they are in partnership with the pastor. They are not sheep who need the shepherd to do the wrangling.

It is a powerful spiritual discipline for a congregation to lower its expectations of a pastor and discover that anyone can make a hospital call and anyone can lead a prayer. Returning to a partnership model will restore health in the congregation.

Clergy burnout also occurs when the pastor fails to take the necessary time and attention for self-care and prayer. Trying to live up to others' expectations is usually a key reason a pastor fails at this. Who has time for rest and prayer if they are expected to be on call all the time? We believe clergy and leadership fatigue, as well as a general lack of health in a church, contributes largely to why seekers reject church as a venue for their spiritual growth.

We long for churches to become spiritual communities that feed the hunger of the people by meeting them where they are and for everyone in a congregation, not just the pastor or those on the leadership team, to be an important spiritual leader. In the book of Isaiah, the prophet writes to address the Israelites exactly where they are as they faced captivity in Babylon. God extends to Israel an invitation to travel home to Jerusalem and begin again. But first God says to them, "Incline your ear, and come to me; listen, so that you may live" (55:3). In a time when the church is seeking to find its way in a confusing and complex ethos, the invitation to "incline our ears" to hear God is of critical importance.

## ABOUT THIS BOOK

*Incline Your Ear* seeks to bring to the heart of the church the principles and practices that spiritual directors have known and taught for centuries. Spiritual direction, as it is usually practiced and taught, has four areas of emphasis:

- Becoming more aware of the presence of the Holy in our daily lives

- Reflecting on that awareness and deepening in our relationship with God
- Discerning where God is leading
- Sharing our spiritual gifts with the world

*Incline Your Ear* will address these four areas, touching on what they mean both for individuals and for churches. We will share principles, spiritual practices to experience, and processes to follow in a sequence as a kind of road map to becoming a spiritual community. In addition, there will be some simple ways for communities to evaluate their spiritual growth.

This road map is designed to move churches from awareness to action. The destination is discovering how God is calling you and your church to share your gifts in the world. You may think you already know the answer to that, and perhaps you do. We challenge you to go back to the basics, starting with cultivating or deepening an awareness of God in your daily life and in the life of your church community. We'll move from there to a number of ways to reflect on that awareness and remember the goodness we have received from God. Then it's on to the ancient and rich tradition of spiritual discernment—sifting and sorting through facts, insights, and nudges in prayer to discover the path of God's wisdom for you and your church. Then, in the chapter on sharing our spiritual gifts with the world, we will discover some wonderful tools of contemplative listening and sharing that will empower everyone in your congregation to listen "from the heart." This chapter is designed to take an enormous burden off overworked church leaders as everyone learns how to listen and care for—without fixing or rescuing—another person.

Taking this journey in sequence will be a joy-filled, life-giving process for your congregation. You can take the segments at your own pace and spend as much time as you need with each one before moving forward. If you are the pastor, you can incorporate elements of whatever chapter you are on into sermons, newsletters, and other forms of congregational communication. Leaders of church boards may use the suggested spiritual practices during meetings. Small groups may want to do the same thing. Church educators can use the book for study, discussing each segment as the church works through the journey together. Individuals can do the spiritual practices at home alone or with their friends and family.

Our hope is that if communities of faith study and experience *Incline Your Ear* together, they will find new ways to be in love with God and listen to the Spirit. Then pastors don't have to do it all; the members will be equipped to share their gifts with one another. The moderator can rest in the peace of knowing that the board has discerned the vision well. And church members can still enjoy their yoga while discovering that Christianity has a rich buffet of spiritual food as well. The invitation that God gave the Israelites in the time of Babylonian captivity was to "Incline your ear . . . listen, so that you may live." Such an invitation is before *us*, to embrace the ancient Christian practices of listening and discernment, so that we as the church may live. Come, let us listen together.

## ACKNOWLEDGMENTS

No book is ever written in isolation. We are shaped by the writers who came before us in our field, and we are shaped by the spiritual pilgrims who have molded our worldview and spiritual journeys. We write in the shadows of mentors, college and seminary professors, friends, family, colleagues, pastors, poets, theologians, and mystics. Inasmuch as we have been shaped by these spheres of influence, we pray this book will offer wisdom and encouragement to the many who seek to live into the hard work of the spiritual life.

## CHAD R. ABBOTT

This book is grounded in the exploration of the spiritual life, and it seems appropriate to name the community that has surrounded me in my own journey and without whom this book could never have been written. I am forever indebted to Craig Boyd, Brian Hartley, Ruth Huston, Rick McPeak, and Jim Reinhard from my time at Greenville College. Because of their infinite wisdom in helping ground my spirituality in a "faith seeking understanding" framework, I continue to listen for God in my life. While in seminary, I came across some of the most influential people I will ever meet and for which my journey would never be the same. The vision in these pages comes from their insistent reminder that my voice matters. Among these colleagues are Jonathan Walton, Gregory Ellison II, Sarah Griffith Lund, Erica Smith Thompson, Tim Kennedy, Mike and Amber Neuroth, Noelle and John Tennis Gulden, Ryan and Alicia Taylor Byers, and Everett Mitchell. I continue to be shaped by places of study as I finish my doctoral work at Christian Theological Seminary. I am so grateful for the guidance of Dr. Scott Seay, Dr. Helene Russell, Dr. Dick Hamm, Dr. Bill Kincaid, and Dean Leah Gunning-Francis.

I am also shaped by faith communities where I have served, worshipped, or studied over the years. I am so thankful to the fine folks at Broadway United Methodist Church in Indianapolis, whose ongoing support of me during a time of uncertainty has given shape to my journey in ways that are unexplainable: From Mike Mather to Duane Carlisle, the larger staff and laity that I consider friends and colleagues. My faith journey has changed and will never be the same. I am profoundly and forever grateful for my first United Church of Christ congregation, Saint Paul's Church in Alexandria, Kentucky. This church helped me heal and find joy in serving as pastor. Without their persistent belief in God's call upon my life, I might have never written this book.

In my current home congregation, I cannot help but thank my senior pastor, Rev. Lori Bievenour, for her wisdom, understanding, and support of me as I entered into the work of middle judicatory ministry. Both Lori and the wider congregation of Saint Peter's UCC in Carmel, Indiana, continue to shape my life as a person of faith. Additionally, my current setting of ministry in the Indiana-Kentucky Conference has offered me so much space to discover how important this book really is to the life of the church. What a joy it is to serve the many UCC churches and pastors in Indiana and Kentucky. I am so blessed to know and serve alongside Rebecca Braganza, Monica Ouellette, Toni Hawkins, Val Ruess, Nicole Shaw, and a supportive board of directors. I also give God thanks for the many colleagues in the Council of Conference Ministers in the UCC, among them David Ackerman, Bonnie Bates, Shana Johnson, Mike Denton, Brigit Stevens, Shari Prestemon, Gordon Rankin, David Long-Higgins, Kent Siladi, Edith Guffey, Franz Rigert, John Vertigan, Lee Albertson, Freeman Palmer, Ginny Brown Daniels, Deborah Blood, Ed Davis, Sue Artt, Diane Wieble, Bill Lyons, and our general minister and president, John Dorhauer.

The work of spiritual friendships is an ongoing place of nurture for me and one in which I cannot ignore in light of a book on spirituality. I give thanks for the many soul friends who have shaped me in profound ways, including Ken Weidinger, Keith Haithcock, Ryan Taylor Byers, Alicia Taylor Byers, Beth Long-Higgins, Darrel Goodwin, Jeff Gallagher, Courtney Stange-Tregear, Elizabeth Dilley, Jill Olds, Nicole Havelka, Leah Robberts-Mosser, Michelle Torigian, Desiree Gold, Danny Walker, Greg Pimlott, Dave and Jamalyn Williamson, Lisa Schubert Nowling, Cindy Wood, my sister Megan Schultz, and Noelle and John Tennis Gulden.

Given that this is a book on spiritual direction, I need to thank my direction community. I give God thanks for my spiritual director, Judy Fackenthal; the sisters at the Our Lady of Grace Monastery in Indianapolis, who have taught me so much; my classmates in the class of 2016 Hesychia School of Spiritual Direction; and my classmates in the Spiritual Direction Internship at the Benedict Inn.

I am grateful for such an amazing writing partner in Teresa Blythe. Writing this book with you, Teresa, has been a joy, and I look forward to all that unfolds in the wider United Church of Christ as we work together.

Finally, I would be amiss if I didn't mention my family. Thank you to my two kids, Isabel and Solomon, and my wife, Shannon, whose unwavering support has made this journey possible. Thank you for telling me to keep writing. Thank you to our Godfamily, Alicia, Ryan, Gus, and Gabriel, for always holding me in prayer. Thank you to my parents, Marilyn and Marty Abbott; my siblings, Eric and Megan; and all my extended family. Discernment is not just a solitary act, but the work of a community of spiritual pilgrims. Thank you, spiritual family, for helping make this book possible.

## TERESA BLYTHE

When I graduated from seminary in 2000 and set out to do spiritual-direction work full-time, I had high hopes that if churches simply learned about spiritual disciplines and discernment, then they would all thrive and grow (church growth being everyone's goal at the time). Believing growth was linked to spiritual vitality and that the practice of discernment was crucial to spiritual vitality, I set out, with great enthusiasm, to "educate" mostly mainline churches and denominations about this age-old practice. I had much to learn and—with few takers—time to learn it. But I kept the faith and connected with other spiritual professionals who also believed that the principles of spiritual direction and discernment could draw our church communities closer to God in concrete and exciting ways. And out of that network, we all began to experiment with working in congregations in much the same way as we would work in spiritual direction with individuals.

These connections include many spiritual directors, professors, and pastors who taught and supported me over the years in what I call "organizational spiritual direction." My first exposure to the concept was in Br. Jack Mostyn's Systems and Structures class for the Diploma in the Art of Spiritual Direction program at San Francisco Theological Seminary (SFTS).

In fact, most everything I know about discernment stems from classes I took at SFTS from 1997 to 2000 under my esteemed professor, Dr. Elizabeth Liebert. She taught an Ignatian process that I think is better than any other I've encountered anywhere (and there are a lot to choose from). I have been teaching and using the process for years, so much so that it's in my bones and in my heart. I have attempted to use my own words and speak my own truth about discernment and to credit Dr. Liebert as appropriate, but because I was so deeply shaped by her work, I might on occasion unintentionally use words or phrases I learned from her. In addition, I have used the process she taught in the Diploma in the Art of Spiritual Direction program as the foundation for the process I'm sharing in the road map in chapter 4. I'm grateful to Dr. Liebert for her inspirational work and recommend her book, *The Way of Discernment*, for a detailed and expanded process of Ignatian discernment.

Other professionals who paved the way for this work include Dr. Nancy Wiens; Mark Yaconelli and the Youth Ministry & Spirituality Project, 2000; Dr. Paul Anderson of the George Fox University Congregational Discernment Project of 2009; and all the participants of the Volunteers Exploring Vocation venture of the Fund for Theological Studies. I continue to be grateful for the work I do with Greg Essenmacher and the Sacred Transformation Group and for the support of my personal and vocational "dream team": Fr. Greg Wiest, Rev. Canon Greg Foraker, Rev. Kay Collette, Rev. Elizabeth Nordquist, the late Rev. Dina Gardner, Rev. Dr. Gil Stafford, Rev. Brandon Wert, Sara Meza, Shawna Hansen, and Rev. Teresa Cowan Jones.

While work done with individual churches is confidential, I am grateful to the many Presbyterian (USA), United Church of Christ (UCC), and Disciples of Christ (Christian) churches that have hired me over the years to facilitate spiritual growth and discernment. My own church, First UCC Phoenix, likes to think of itself as a test group for new ideas I come up with, and I'm delighted to be of service! Many thanks to Pastors James Pennington and Susan Valiquette for their support. And it's great to have colleagues like the general minister and president of the United Church of Christ, Rev. Dr. John Dorhauer, cheering us on as we write about one of his favorite subjects.

I am deeply indebted to the Hesychia School of Spiritual Direction in Tucson, where I spent fourteen years directing and teaching—and where I met a young UCC pastor and now conference minister, Chad Abbott, who was just as excited about organizational spiritual direction as I. Our conversations about the needs of congregations and how spiritual directors might meet those needs fueled this project. Thank you, Chad, for suggesting we put our heads together on this. Whoever describes writing as easy? But it has been easy to write this with you.

The writings of Diana Butler Bass, Parker Palmer, Richard Rohr, and other giants in the field of Christian spirituality provide a strong foundation for this book, though to be fair, there are bookcases full of excellent writing by lesser-known authors I could mention if I had the space.

And finally, my deepest gratitude to my husband, Duane

Schneider, whose positive attitude and appreciation of this mystical, spiritual work I do keeps me at it even when I get discouraged.

## CHAD AND TERESA

We both wish to extend our gratitude to Beth Gaede and the folks at Fortress Press for working with us on this project. We know that this book is critical for the future of the church, and we know that you have seen this vision, too. Thank you for taking this book to print.

# Introduction

In a world full of solutions, opinions, and advice, the listening ear is one of the most important gifts we can offer one another. It is an act of healing and vision. We believe that for people of faith and their communities, the gift of listening both to one another and God offers individuals a path to spiritual renewal and grants congregations a vision of their identity. In a time when congregations are in steep decline and facing significant uncertainty, learning to listen deeply to one another, and seeking through listening to discern God's path for a faith community's future, just might be one of the most important acts a church can engage.

We two authors minister in a denomination that believes "God is still speaking." The phrase is more than a slogan or a denominational campaign. It expresses the reality that God is much more mysterious and far-reaching than we can understand. While the Bible continues to serve as the primary source of revelation for Christians, God is still being revealed to us in this world, in a culture the ancient world could not have imagined. As our good friend Rev. Mike Mather is fond of saying, "God didn't stop speaking just because the book went to press." Thus, if God is still speaking, we need to find a way to listen deeply, to "listen with the ears of our heart," as Saint Benedict of Nursia has said.

We love Benedict's notion of listening with more than our ears. While modern medicine views the heart primarily as a vital organ in the body, the heart as metaphor carries even greater weight. Phrases such as "take heart" and "speak from the heart," learning something "by heart," and having a "heart-to-heart" conversation all point to the understanding that the heart is the seat of the emotions. In ancient Egypt, people believed that the human soul was made up of many different parts of the body, but the key to the soul and to the afterlife was the heart, for it was the seat of emotion, will, and intention. The heart is a metaphor for our deepest passions, our longing for community and belonging, particularly with the Divine. With the heart as such a powerful metaphor in our understanding of community and belonging, Benedict was right to urge us to listen with the ears of our heart.

Science also leads us toward some profound spiritual and theological insights. The human heart is one of only two organs in our body that both give and receive. The heart pumps blood to the entire body, giving us life, and blood also flows back into the heart. Without this flow, we would not survive. The only other organ in the body that does this is the lungs, which receive air, transferring oxygen into our blood, and expelling carbon dioxide. No wonder the biblical writers use the metaphors of breath and heart (Ps 150:6; Matt 22:37), because in these very things is life. We understand that our relationship with God is one of giving and receiving, which requires a different kind of listening.

As spiritual directors, our primary work is helping a directee or a group pay attention to this flow of receiving and giving in our relationship with God. In *Candlelight: Illuminating the Art of Spiritual Direction*, spiritual director Susan Phillips argues that lighting a candle at the beginning of each session offers us a reminder to awaken to the work of listening and attuning one's spiritual sensibilities to God. Phillips says, "Spiritual directors, by skill and vocation, help people notice and cultivate ways of knowing and being known by God."[1] Noticing and knowing God depend on training one's spiritual ear to hear with the ear of our heart. We understand listening as an act of inclining the ear of the heart to receive and give in our relationship with God.

The notion of listening is closely related to the concept of discernment, which we will address in chapter 3. While discernment is not only a matter of listening for God, listening certainly is a significant part of the discernment process. Listening and discernment work together, with listening being the attuning of our spiritual ears to hear from God, and discernment being the practice of noticing where God's spirit is especially alive and taking action. As the reader will uncover in our chapter on discernment, it is the sifting and sorting of information, feelings, insights, intuition, beliefs, and values, so we can make faithful choices in all of life. *The goal of spiritual discernment is to make choices that will result in a deeper relationship with God.* You may find us referring to both listening and discernment in this book, and while they are not the same, they are certainly both needed for cultivating spiritual awakening within congregations.

## CONGREGATIONAL LISTENING

Learning to listen is critical not just for individuals, but for churches as spiritual communities. Sadly, it is evident to us as leaders in the mainline American church that many Christians do not know how to listen for God, in spite of their deep longing to connect with a God who still speaks. Just as individual Christians struggle to listen for God, faith communities labor to listen for God together. Thus, the question this book addresses is, how does a congregation listen for God?

Throughout this book, we will be sharing spiritual practices designed to help your congregation "incline its ear" toward God. Notice we used the singular *ear.* We believe congregations need to understand themselves as unified—one body, rather than a collection of individuals. Certainly, individuals can and should use the spiritual practices we write about, and the practices are easily adapted for that purpose. The more individuals experience the value of regular spiritual practices, the easier it is for the congregation to do the practices together. But the primary focus for this book is the congregation (or a body representing the congregation, such as a board or leadership team) and how it can listen for God with the ear of its heart.

While the aim of churches, synagogues, mosques, and sanghas is to create sacred space where people can experience the Holy, a modern paradox seems to resist this effort. While churches and other religious bodies seek to engage people's spiritual longings, people are increasingly less likely to seek spiritual nourishment in a community of faith. In 2019, a Pew Research study found that the number of people who describe themselves as Christian had dropped nearly 12 percent in the past decade. Equally troubling is that the percentage of those who identify as unaffiliated with any religious body increased by 17 percent in that same ten-year period.[2] Even more interesting to those of us working in religious systems is that while the number of people involved in faith communities continues to decline, another group of pilgrims who identify as "spiritual but not religious" is growing rapidly (17 percent in 2019, up from 12 percent in 2009). In other words, we are back to our preface's reminder that many people find God on their yoga mat or in the woods or while running a marathon, rather than in a traditional church community.

This paradox may seem perplexing, perhaps counterintuitive, to an average churchgoer. But to those who identify as "spiritual but not religious" or who have moved away from mainline or evangelical churches or religious institutions of any kind, these shifts in the places where people experience God come as no surprise. Spiritual seekers who are not church members and who do not regularly attend worship express a deep longing for connection with the Divine, but they are just not finding that in a traditional church. They seek something ancient, something that gets at the root of what it means to be human.

The irony, of course, is that the word *religion*, a word so quickly tossed aside these days, means literally "to get back to the root." So while many have chosen to leave churches or not affiliate with any religious body, the longing for rich and deep spirituality—an experience of connection with a sense of Wholeness that is bigger than ourselves—has not gone away, and it may be on the rise. Therefore, a working assumption in this book is that one of the reasons churches have lost so many members is that we as the church have failed to offer people a spiritual path that connects with where they are and with the questions that spring from the very heart of their being. We have sought to maintain a sacred institution rather than open doors and mark pathways for church members to experience the Sacred itself.

The questions that spring from the heart of those seeking God both inside and outside of the church provide us with much to consider. Such seekers might ask, "Who am I? Is there something I am called to live out in my life? How will I know what my calling is, and will it always be the same throughout my entire life? Who are the pilgrims that will journey with me as I seek answers to my spiritual questions?" But we have neither offered spiritually rich practices to help people address the questions they bring to church nor gone outside the church to meet our neighbors and hear their questions. No wonder people have left faith communities for the yoga mat, the woods, and the running trails. What is more, seminaries have not prepared clergy to guide congregations in the deep work of listening for God. Clergy and laity have been taught how to lead prayer in corporate worship, but few of us have been trained to discern, to listen, or to enter into the contemplative life, and we now see the effect this is having not only on leaders, but also on the willingness of people to participate in congregational life.

The world outside our church doors will not wait around for clergy to figure out how to connect contemplative life with congregational life, so explorers turn to yoga studios, meditation mats, healing stones, and spirituality apps—and who can blame them? Yet, the church has a deep and abiding tradition of spiritual practices that can help spiritual pilgrims in our time get to the heart of their yearning. In particular, the work of spiritual direction going back to the desert fathers and mothers has the potential not only to enhance spiritual vitality in the church, but also to push us toward congregational vitality that helps churches more fully live out their mission during the world in a time when a vibrant church is desperately needed. Before we explore how such practices in the Christian tradition can transform the church, however, we must set a biblical and theological foundation for what we mean by inclining our ear to listen for God.

## OUR BIBLICAL AND THEOLOGICAL FOUNDATION

The two of us long for churches to become spiritual communities that feed the hunger of the people by meeting them where they are and to become communities where everyone in a congregation, not just the pastor or those on the leadership team, is a spiritual leader. In the book of Isaiah, the prophet addresses the Israelites exactly where they are—in captivity in Babylon. God extends to Israel an invitation to travel home to Jerusalem and restore their community in their homeland. But first, God says to them, "Incline your ear, and come to me; listen, so that you may live" (55:3). In a confusing and complex time when the church is seeking to find its way, the invitation to "incline your ear" to God can lead both congregations and individual seekers into renewal.

Throughout Scripture, God repeatedly calls for the people of God to incline their ear, to listen. All along the journey, God offers them the intimacy of relationship and connection. The giving-and-receiving relationship of the heart between God and the people, which we introduced in the opening paragraphs of this introduction, is an ongoing theme of the biblical narratives. Moses hears the voice of God in the burning bush, which leads to guide the Israelites from Egypt to freedom. God calls Samuel three times, and Samuel responds, "Here I am, for you called me" (1 Sam 3:6). God tells Elijah to go up Mount Horeb and wait for God to pass by. As Elijah waits, a strong wind, an earthquake, and even fire occur, but God is not in any of these. Finally, there is silence, and out of the silence God calls upon Elijah to return to the wilderness of Damascus. The angel Gabriel comes to Mary to tell her that she will conceive a child. He remarks, "Do not be afraid, Mary, for you have found favor with God. And now, you will conceive in your womb and bear a son, and you will name him Jesus" (Luke 1:30–32). She replies, "How can this be, since I am a virgin?" (v. 34). After Gabriel explains that the child will come through the Holy Spirit and that nothing is impossible with God, Mary responds, "Here am I, the servant of the Lord; let it be with me according to your word" (v. 38). In Jesus's ministry, he admonishes his followers to listen. For example, the parable of the sower ends, "As he said this, he called out, 'Let anyone with ears to hear listen'" (Luke 8:8).

In the classic Hebrew *shema* (*shema* means "hear"), a prayer from Deuteronomy 6 that is part of Jewish morning and evening prayers, the opening words remind us to listen: "Hear, O Israel! The Lord is our God, the Lord alone. You shall love the Lord your God with all of your heart and with all of your soul and with all your might" (vv. 4–5). As we ponder what it means for us to incline our ear to God, these texts and others like them provide a starting point for understanding the role of listening in the community of God. Listening, however, is not just a practical matter; it is a theological framework.

Theology is not about only the beliefs that are embedded in us. It is the way we understand God's mission in the world. Based upon the mission of God, we arrive at laying this foundation with a few basic theological assumptions to ground us. This language and framework for God assumes the church still has something to offer the spiritual pilgrim and the local congregation as they incline their ear toward God.

### Assumption 1: God Is as Close to Us as Our Very Breath

A theological foundation for spiritual discernment and listening in individual faith and corporate or congregational faith is rooted in the idea that God is near and that we exist within God. Psalm 139 reminds us of the nearness of God:

> Where can I go from your spirit?
>     Or where can I flee from your presence?
> If I ascend to heaven, you are there;
>     if I make my bed in Sheol, you are there.
> If I take the wings of the morning
>     and settle at the farthest limits of the sea,
> even there your hand shall lead me,
>     and your right hand shall hold me fast. (7–10)

Additionally, the opening pages of Genesis attest that the work of creation emanates from God and that human beings are made in the very image of God, indicating that while we are not God, we are made in God's likeness and therefore interconnected with all other beings, both human and nonhuman. What is more, Jesus says he and God "are one." In fact, in John 17 he prayed that we all would be one with each other, just as he and God are one. The book of Acts also reminds us that God is so near to us that in God, we "live and move and have our being" (17:28).

That we are interconnected with creation and God and made in the very image of God should be reflected in the spiritual life. The spiritual life is not a process of conjuring up a God from some distant land or dimension to meet our needs. It is an awakening to a God of love that is already present and still speaking in the world and in our lives. Spiritual practices, including discernment and spiritual direction, help us notice where God is speaking, moving, and transforming. Spiritual discernment is a movement toward a greater awareness of our place within God and how God is moving us toward transformation and renewal. Therefore, our first assumption grounds us in a God of nearness and intimate relationship, a giving-and-receiving relationship held up by and centered in a love beyond measure.

## Assumption 2: The Story of God
## and Humanity in Relationship Is Still Unfolding

The spiritual life is a movement toward a greater awareness of our relationship to God. It is also an awakening to our mutual story with God and its unfolding in the present. We recall from earlier in this introduction that this relationship with God is one of giving and receiving, which means our mutual story with God is not static. Loving relationships embody a willingness to be shaped by the other as our stories unfold. The nature of the connection between God and creation is not predetermined but rather reflects the dynamism found in all relationships—a dance between partners in which each one responds to the movements of the other. God's primary movement in relationship with us and creation is one of love and compassion, even in the midst of suffering, oppression, and injustice. Theologian Jay McDaniel writes in his book *Of God and Pelicans*, "If we take the love that

Jesus strove to embody, if we imaginatively extend its breadth and depth beyond limit, and if we then envision that breadth and depth as gathered into the unity of a single, universal Consciousness, we have an image of God. Whatever else it is, we trust that the divine Mystery is a wellspring of unlimited love."[3]

The power of this movement in God's unlimited love with us is such that spiritual discernment and listening to God can awaken us to God's love for the world. Thus, the focus of the spiritual life is to incline our ear—to listen deeply to and look closely at all of our experiences of the world, for God is present to us in all things. Those who are listening for God, then, are not afraid to ask hard questions and sit in the not-knowing because they understand that sometimes the answers are still unfolding along with our relationship to God. Such listening takes place within a liminal space between what God has already done in history and what is yet to unfold. The spiritual life is not a journey toward pie in the sky or an apocalypse or some other vision of the end times. God is present in our midst right now, and spiritual listening attunes our spiritual senses in such a way that we can be awake to God's ever-present love in our lives and in creation around us. Therefore, we assume a God who is near and a God whose story is interconnected with our own and unfolding.

## Assumption 3: God Invites Us
## to Be Renewed

Our third theological assumption is that as we tend to the unfolding of our stories and God's story, God invites us to be renewed, to deepen the original connection God made with us in our creation. We are each created a beloved child of God, and God yearns for us to live into God's vision of us as God's beloved. Renewal allows for God to restore our broken images, our sins, and our waywardness. Renewal allows for us to reclaim our own vision of ourselves as beloved in the eyes of God. And such a renewal has the power to transform lives and even whole communities.

Our spiritual journey is a movement with God toward the likeness of Christ. Through the work of the Holy Spirit, we are assured that the Risen Christ—indeed, God—has always been and continues to be present in the world. Such a notion of transformation or renewal does not assume that because a Christian is "saved," they possess something another person does not. Such theology creates an us-and-them dichotomy that can be dangerous, presumptuous, and exclusive. Our understanding of renewal is that God is at work in all people and that when we talk with others about matters of faith, we must avoid assuming that we are enlightened and the other person is not. Rather, we must be awake to the reality that all are beloved in the eyes of God. It is our assumption that God is at work within all people and in all of creation, moving us toward embodying the love and compassion of Christ.

These assumptions are the foundation for becoming discerning and spiritually alive individuals and congregations. They invite us into a deeper relationship with God. The invitation is ours to take, if we will but attune our senses to God's presence in the world. With each important decision we make, with every relationship we build, with every church mission statement or ministry we design, and in matters of vocation and prophetic witness, the skills of discernment and listening in the spiritual life will make for vital congregations. While we face declining membership and generational shifts in loyalty to the church, it is clear to us that the present is both a challenging and exciting time to be the church. We have the opportunity to imagine a new future as we listen for God's leading. All the spiritual resources we need to be that newly imagined and future church are already within and around us if we will but incline our ear to the work of the Spirit.

## THE WIDER VISION

In the remainder of this book, we will explore the four movements of listening for God as practiced in classic spiritual direction and how these movements relate to the vitality of congregations. We will begin in chapter 1 with the development of awareness as a key practice for beginning to listen for God. The chapter concludes with the first segment of the Congregational Spiritual Road Map, which will be extended at the end of each chapter. We suggest your leadership team or small groups use the road map to guide the development of your awareness and capacity to listen deeply. In chapter 2, we will learn to reflect on, to savor, our awareness. Chapter 3 will shift to discernment, the link between awareness or contemplation and action. In chapter 4, we will explore how making decisions and acting based on discernment can renew congregations. In fact, we believe these movements of listening and discernment can activate deep spiritual renewal and vitality that are clearly missing in today's mainline and evangelical churches. Congregations will see a new path in the wilderness if they will be attuned and awakened to the Spirit in their midst.

After describing these four essential movements of spiritual direction, we will focus on how this model in congregations is connected to the larger work of social justice in churches. We are convinced that the hard work of listening and discernment is essential to creating a just world for all. Contemplation and social justice work together, so chapter 5 will address this connection and how congregations embody both. In closing, we will unpack how this movement of spiritual listening and discernment is the very foundation of the future church as we see it.

While this book offers wisdom for the renewal of God's church, we in no way believe that our approach will solve all of the challenges of the mainline and evangelical churches in America. However, we do hope that this way of seeing and practicing faith can lead us to hear more clearly how God is leading congregations to a renewal of mission and vision for building a just world for all. If this book offers even a glimmer of such renewal, then it will have been worth the time learning what it means to incline our ear.

*1*

## Awareness of God

Be still, and know that I am God!
  I am exalted among the nations,
  I am exalted in the earth.
—Psalm 46:10

The first step in becoming a spiritual community is cultivating awareness of God. Understanding where and how the Spirit is moving and how to share that understanding is the first task we will explore in this journey.

Sadly, clergy and laity in some congregations carry an unspoken fear of talking about how individuals, much less how congregations, experience God. Even while we may say with the Psalmist, "It is good to be near God" (Ps 73:28), we may harbor fears or insecurities about what being near God means. Perhaps we were brought up with a punitive image of God and know we have work to do on that image. Or we may sense that drawing near to God means taking on responsibilities we don't feel ready to assume. Or we may simply not know where to start.

We don't have to let this insecurity hold us back. Time-honored practices received from the early church mothers and fathers show us how to safely and confidently draw closer to the One who is nearer to us than our very breath. To grow spiritually, we need to spend time in these practices as individuals and as congregations. Furthermore, we need to talk about our experiences so we understand we are not alone nor are we unusual in either our ecstasy or our frustration as we stumble toward awareness of God.

Awareness of God grows through forms of prayer, reflection, and times of meditation or as a result of sharing our spiritual life with a trusted, nonjudgmental person, such as a spiritual director or mentor. If a congregation is not supporting intentional spiritual practice, the congregation will have difficulty growing in spiritual vitality.

Awareness of God is not the same as belief in God. Prayer, meditation, and discernment practices are tools handed to us by our Christian ancestors, and these spiritual teachers meant for them to be used regularly by all the people of God in worship and in daily life. How we use these tools varies, but they are useless if we keep them on a shelf.

## AWARENESS IS A MULTIFAITH PURSUIT

All the major religious traditions of the world teach the importance of awareness of the Transcendent. In many Eastern traditions, people practice a form of meditation to simply be in the presence of the Holy. Zen Buddhists sit in silence for long periods of time to cleanse the mind of attachments and cravings. Hindus practice *samadhi*, which means "the bliss from transcending the mind" and is a type of yoga utilizing deep breathing and simple postures. Sufi Muslims call their contemplative prayer *fana*, or "mystical communion with the Divine."

In our pluralistic world, we find a multitude of books promoting a variety of ways to meditate for increased awareness, a practice commonly called mindfulness. One of the most popular has been Eckhart Tolle's *The Power of Now: A Guide to Spiritual Enlightenment*. Tolle, along with many psychologists, spiritual leaders, and medical professionals, urges us to spend some quiet time each day directly experiencing the present moment—refraining from thinking about the past or the future, settling quietly in the *now*, and simply observing what is. A good, nonreligious explanation of the value of spending time in this "direct experience" is found in David Rock's *Your Brain at Work*. Rock, a leadership coach, says our ability to concentrate and overcome distraction increases as we spend time each day in "direct experience."[1] Doing this involves choosing a sense (sight, sound, touch, taste, or smell) and focusing attention just on that one sense for a short period of time. This direct-experience exercise builds concentration and helps enormously as people prepare to try contemplative forms of prayer.

Turning our attention to the present moment, we become fully alive to that moment. That is where we meet God. Many theologians and spiritual teachers argue that the present moment is all we ever have. Yet how often do we stay there? We are so geared to think ahead, troubleshoot, strategically plan, and obsess or to dwell on hurts or mistakes and events in the past that we spend precious little time in the moment.

A congregation that seeks to be a spiritual community needs to spend time *together* in the moment. There is a time and place for attending to the past and future, such as during discernment and strategic planning, but in the daily life of the church, the most important moment is "now."

## GOOD NEWS: YOU'VE ALREADY BEGUN

This chapter offers some practices to help your congregation grow in awareness of the presence of God. But before we turn to these practices, it is important to note that your congregation already has awareness of God. But perhaps members do not yet name it as such.

If we believe that we find God in all things and all places, then we know that each of us has experienced the power and spirit of God. A chief part of spiritual leaders' work in a community is to assist people in uncovering their own awareness of the Holy. Here's some of the language people use to describe how they experience God, even though they may not yet name what they feel as an experience of God:

- I find that every time I go running, my mind seems to clear, and I find insight for whatever problem I'm working on.

- When my baby smiles and looks me right in the eyes, I just melt and feel incredibly alive.

- Something about that photograph of the destruction of the earthquake moved me to appreciate my life even more.

- Looking out over the Grand Canyon, I felt at one with the universe.

- I was so grateful for that good report from the doctor that I sang all the way home.

- I feel a presence, a loving presence, every time I speak out against injustice.

- The love I feel for my partner is beyond all my understanding. It feels eternal.

None of those statements mentions God, yet each describes what can be seen as an experience of God. People today are cautious about using too much religious language—and for good reason. They may have been abused by people who hurt them in the name of God. They may feel so humbled by their experience of an unseen reality that they do not feel qualified to name it as an experience of God. Our religious language is too small to adequately express some of these experiences. That's OK. We don't have to invoke God's name all the time to speak about the Holy. We find God in the places in our life where we experience

Deep love
Longing
Transcendence
Insight
Life
Presence
Gratitude
Patience
Kindness
Joy
Peace

The list could go on, but you get the idea. When we pay attention to the attributes of God or the fruit of the Spirit that Paul outlines (Gal 5:22–23), we develop "eyes to see and ears to hear" where God's Spirit is moving in the world.

## BIBLICAL NOTIONS OF AWARENESS

In introducing awareness, we have already mentioned the influence of Eastern thought and philosophy, and you may be wondering about a Christian basis for increasing awareness. It is found in the Bible.

Writings in the Hebrew Scriptures invite us to an embodied spirituality, a faith that takes seriously our bodies as well as our minds and spirits. They speak of human beings made in the image of God (Gen 1:26–27), and we are told that God's ways are already planted in our hearts. We don't have to reach to the heavens to know God! "No, the word is very near to you; it is in your mouth and in your heart to observe" (Deut 30:14). We can see it, if we are looking. We can also hear it. The writer of Isaiah urges us to "pay attention to the little voice." When you turn to the right or when you turn to the left, your ears shall hear a word behind you, saying, "This is the way; walk in it" (Isa 30:21).

Jesus constantly called people to awareness of what is true in their lives. In Luke's summary of Jesus's teaching, the Sermon on the Plain, we hear Jesus asking, "Why do you see the speck in your neighbor's eye but do not notice the log in your own eye?" (Luke 6:41). Jesus wants us awake and watchful: "Be dressed for action and have your lamps lit" (Luke 12:35). The many stories of Jesus restoring sight to people who were blind indicate not only his compassion for people who cannot see, but also his passion for eradicating spiritual blindness.

Paul's letter to the Romans also includes a call to awakening: "You know what time it is, how it is now the moment for you to wake from sleep" (Rom 13:11). He's summoning the church in Rome to peaceful and moral action—to "see the light."

So the call to awareness is certainly not exclusive to Eastern religions.

## CHRISTIAN MYSTICISM

In the Western church, contemplative practices to enhance awareness seem new because they were uncommon for centuries, used mainly by contemplative and mystic Catholics. This changed in the twentieth century with a resurgence of interest in centering prayer—wordless, imageless, silent prayer. Experimentation with prayer beyond words led to a greater interest in some of the third- and fourth-century Christian mystics—the Desert Fathers and Mothers in Egypt, Palestine, and Syria. Writings such as *Sayings of the Desert Fathers* indicate that these early Christians left their cities and towns for an austere life where they might confront their demons and be filled with the

Holy Spirit. They were reacting to the institutionalization of the church and were determined to create a new society.

People followed these holy men and women to the desert to consult with them and to receive "a word" from the master. This might be only one word, a phrase, or a sentence, but it was spiritual food to chew over and savor. The Desert Fathers and Mothers were known for advising people to take time away from hurried city life. One of the most famous sayings is from Abba Moses (from fourth-century Egypt), who told a pilgrim to "sit in your cell, and your cell will teach you everything," implying that the full meaning of the life of the Spirit would be revealed in solitude and silence.[2] In fact, these hermits chose the desert as home because they understood that the starkness of the desert strips away our illusions and pretensions, leaving us with only ourselves and God. From the Desert Fathers and Mothers came the monastic movement, as many of them banded together to form working communities devoted to a life of simplicity and worship.

But mysticism reaches a lot farther than monasticism. A mystic is simply a person captivated by the mystery and wonder of the spiritual realm. Christian mystics feel a special bond with the Holy that defies explanation. Their writings about this bond are more poetry than theology. Some experience a sense of complete union with God; others devote their lives to attaining it. Some who describe themselves as mystics experienced lifelong "visitations" or visions from God, Christ, Mary, or angels. In fact, mystic writer Evelyn Underhill goes so far as to refer to mystical experiences as "the art of union with reality. The mystic is a person who has attained such union in greater or lesser degree; or who aims at and believes in such attainment."[3]

You may not have been raised in a Christian tradition that valued the writings of the mystics, but as you seek Christian grounding for awareness and contemplative prayer practices, you may want to explore the mystics for greater depth. While you may be skeptical about some of their experiences, if you read their writing in a poetic-metaphoric way, you begin to see how they cultivated awareness of God—most of the time through removing themselves from the culture of the day, at least for a period of time, to be in silence and solitude, waiting on God. Four well-known Christian mystics who help us understand the quest for awareness are Julian of Norwich, George Fox, Thomas Merton, and Henri Nouwen.

## JULIAN

Julian of Norwich (1342–1416) lived in a small cell attached to a church in Norwich, England. She wrote about sixteen experiences—or "showings," as she called them—in which she saw God as a nursing mother and Jesus as supreme friend who "shows us our sins by the sweet light of mercy and grace."[4] She writes, "Prayer unites the soul to God, for though the soul may be always like God in nature and in substance restored by grace, it is often unlike him in condition, through sin on man's part. Then prayer is a witness that the soul wills as God wills, and it eases the conscience and fits man for grace."[5]

## GEORGE FOX

George Fox (1624–1691) was a shepherd who in his twenties felt a call to travel the English countryside in search of enlightenment. He had a powerful experience of Christ while on that search: "I heard a voice which said, 'There is one, even Christ Jesus, that can speak to thy condition; and when I heard it my heart did leap for joy."[6]

Fox developed a following of people who wanted direct experience of Christ—which he viewed as the Light within all of us—and began the Society of Friends, also known as Quakers.

To this day, the Quaker way of worship is through silence and waiting for a leading from God.

## THOMAS MERTON

Thomas Merton (1915–1968) was a Trappist monk and writer (*Seven Storey Mountain* is perhaps his best-known book) with a profound influence on contemplative Christian thought today. Merton was highly social yet drawn to solitude and the life of a hermit during certain periods of his life. In his book *Conjectures of a Guilty Bystander,* Merton speaks of a mystical awareness in the center of Louisville, Kentucky's downtown shopping district: "I was suddenly overwhelmed with the realization that I loved all those people, that they were mine and I theirs, that we could not be alien to one another even though we were total strangers. It was like waking from a dream of separateness, of spurious self-isolation in a special world, the world of renunciation and supposed holiness. The whole illusion of a separate holy existence is a dream."[7]

Merton's experience is an excellent example of awareness that hits not during silence or solitude, but from an ordinary moment in daily life. Many mystics believe our time in prayer and contemplation cultivates the soil of our souls, allowing vivid awakenings to emerge at any time or place.

## HENRI NOUWEN

Henri Nouwen (1932–1996) was a Dutch Catholic priest, seminary professor, and prolific writer on contemplative Christian spirituality. Late in his life, Nouwen left a prestigious professor position at Harvard to rest and lead a more ascetic and contemplative life. He spent his last years living and working in the L'Arche community for adults with developmental disabilities. For Nouwen, the "way of the heart" is through solitude, silence, and prayer.

## THE VALUE OF TIME APART

Solitude means pausing from the busyness of life to be with God. It's being alone without being lonely—an intentional time apart in order to listen to the Spirit. Frequently, spiritual seekers find it takes several days of solitude to settle down in order to stop thinking constantly of the past or the future and simply to be in the present. That's why retreats, especially silent ones, are so valuable. They build in time for that letting go period.

But even if you don't have several days to get away, you can experience the benefits of solitude by taking quiet blocks of time in daily life. Some people like to take "hermit days" when they go away to be alone with God. This can be done at a retreat center, a museum, the woods, or in your room (if you can manage to get time away from family or roommates there). Make sure when you take solitude, you allow time to rest in prayer. Certainly, bring your concerns and longings to God in prayer, but also take time to sit back and wait—in silence—to see if insights or leadings emerge. If you practice solitude regularly, you become accustomed to it, and you may desire even more.

One of the purposes of solitude is to help us become silent, which is valuable because, as Nouwen suggests, "silence guards the fire within."[8] It is at this point that extroverts may cry out that Christian spirituality tries to put them into an introverted box, but there really is no way around it—silence opens us to ourselves and to God. And silence has never been solely an introvert's practice.

Think about the world Jesus lived in. No cars and traffic, no cellphones, and no internet. Distractions, to be sure—the reasons Jesus went to places apart. But because we live in a world that feels revved up, bombarding us with distractions, it is important that we take breaks of silence. How can we hear our own wisdom, much less God's wisdom, if we don't take time to shut down the noise of daily life for at least a few minutes? Read any book today on psychological health, spiritual formation, or even success in leadership and you will find advice to take silence and meditation seriously.

The mystics teach us to let go of the notion that we *must* use words in order to pray. Praying with silence is a simple way to practice our unconditional love for God. You are not sitting there expecting something amazing or miraculous to happen. You are with God simply because it is good to be with God, and you are open to God's leading. Many people who practice this form of prayer say that nothing spectacular happens *during* the prayer but that praying this way each day cultivates an awareness throughout the day that allows insights and impressions from God to constantly find ways into their hearts and minds.

We can't emphasize it enough: prayer is at the heart of a relationship with God. You will likely not perceive God's presence and movement in the world if you are not intentionally in contact with God. Similarly, congregations that do not pray miss out on the beauty and power of a living relationship with God.

Imagine if congregations took communal solitude. We are usually such social creatures when we go away with others. If you add times of communal silence to your retreats, you will find out what Quakers have known for centuries: how powerful it is for a spiritual community to sit in silence together, waiting on God and listening for the Spirit's movement.

## MAKING PRAYER IMPORTANT

We're sure that everyone reading this page prays now and then. But we wonder, does your mode of prayer, both individually and congregationally, foster a greater awareness of God? How important do you feel prayer is for you? How important is it in your congregation? If the answer to those last two questions is "not very," don't panic or put yourself or your congregation down. You are not alone.

When Chad was in the Holy Land experiencing pilgrimage, he had a critical awakening to just how much of a challenge prayer can be for a group. They were traveling from Bethlehem to Nazareth and through the Mount of Olives and much of Jerusalem with a Muslim tour guide. The guide noticed the group was not praying, and one morning as they all gathered on the bus for another day of experiencing the biblical lands, he grabbed the bus's microphone and asked, "So, who is going to lead us in prayer this morning? I notice that we haven't been praying, and we really should enter into these moments of discovery through prayer. Who will lead us?" A wave of embarrassment came over Chad and his travel partners. There they were, a group of devoted mainline Protestants, many ordained clergy, and they didn't ground their journey in prayer. It took a person of another faith, one steeped in daily prayer, to remind them that the Christian tradition is also deeply rooted in prayer.

Many churches, especially mainline congregations, turned away from expressive, emotional approaches to prayer and worship in the midtwentieth century to set themselves apart from the more rousing displays by television evangelists and revivalists. We sacrificed the ecstatic experience of God for a more intellectual theological treatment that took seriously biblical scholarship and a commitment to social justice. But that's a sacrifice we don't have to make.

We wouldn't dream of asking your congregation to give up its commitment to biblical scholarship, sound theology, and social justice. In fact, spirituality at its best moves people off their prayer chairs and onto the streets, where they build a just world for all. Contemplation and action go hand in hand. One without the other makes for a lopsided Christian. (We'll have more on that in chapter 5.)

## COMMITTING TO PRAYER

There are so many ways to pray that there really is no excuse for Christians and churches to limit prayer to the few minutes each week when it takes center stage as the "prayers of the people." Instead of offering the rather dry opening and closing prayers at congregational meetings, it would be helpful in congregational settings to intentionally take a "sacred pause" at crucial times during reflection or decision making, drop into silence, and ask, "What is God inviting us to do here?" Imagine what our churches would be like if each individual prayed every day for the life and health of the congregation or if a circle of people felt called to pray for the church on a regular basis.

Throughout this book, we will encourage readers to make a commitment to prayer and meditative practices for developing greater awareness of God. Many prayer practices will be introduced in our Congregational Spiritual Road Map—so many that surely your congregation can find a few that match your personality. We hope congregations will see that prayer is the catalyst of the relationship between them and God. God, of course, initiates the relationship and is there waiting for us. But God doesn't push; rather, God gently waits for us to open ourselves to love by way of prayer.

The important thing to know about cultivating awareness of God is that it takes time. This is not something you will develop overnight, although some spiritual experiences do allow us to take "quantum leaps" from time to time. Give yourself permission to explore this in many ways, and let go of any compulsion you may have to develop a timetable. Don't judge yourself or the congregation for what has not yet developed. Rather, be in the present moment and allow God to meet you where you are. Remember how many times Jesus told people his time had not yet come? Similarly, your time will come on God's timetable. Since you don't know how or when your congregation can clearly point to and articulate an awareness of God's presence, relax and enjoy the journey.

## THE CONGREGATIONAL SPIRITUAL ROAD MAP: EXERCISES TO PREP FOR THE JOURNEY

When we plan for a vacation or a move to a new city, it is helpful to gather information about where we are going. Reading this book is a good start to your journey toward greater awareness of God in your congregation. It's like studying the map before even getting in your vehicle. Prepping well will cultivate a receptivity that is important for our spiritual journey.

We suggest that individuals use the prayer practices and reflections at home alone or with the family and that congregations or small groups within the church use them together.

We recommend spending time after any prayer or relaxation exercise to consider how it has affected you. You may write your responses in a journal. If you are using these practices in a group, use these four open-ended questions to discuss every spiritual practice you do together:

- What did I notice in myself as I was praying (or relaxing)?
- Was this time life-giving, neutral, or upsetting in any way?
- If so, what made it so?
- What invitation has God offered us in our time of prayer?

### PROGRESSIVE RELAXATION

Relaxation is an important prerequisite to prayer. Progressive relaxation is a set of simple tense-and-release exercises that will help you become aware of what muscle tension and relaxation feel like. This exercise promotes health and wholeness while preparing you for prayer or meditation. Follow this simple script to enjoy progressive relaxation:

Sit in a comfortable chair with your feet placed squarely on the floor, or stretch out on a flat surface. If sitting, allow yourself to feel the soles of your feet on the floor, with gravity holding your feet to the ground. Focusing first on the soles of your feet, curl your toes tightly and hold for about five seconds. Release and relax. Tensing and holding, then releasing and relaxing is the heart of progressive relaxation. You will do this with each muscle group, moving up from your feet.

Flex your feet by pointing your toes as far toward you as possible. Hold tightly, then release and relax. Tense your thighs. Hold tightly, then release and relax.

Squeeze your buttocks together. Hold tightly, then release and relax.

Pull in your lower abdomen. Hold tightly, then release and relax.

Cross your arms in front of your chest. Hold tightly, then release and relax.

Clench your fists. Hold tightly, then release and relax.

Pull your fists to your shoulders, tensing your biceps. Hold tightly, then release and relax.

Raise your shoulders to your ears. Hold tightly, then release and relax.

Clench your jaw, and make an angry face. Hold tightly, then release and relax.

Scrunch your face into a tiny ball. Hold tightly, then release and relax.

Look up and tighten your forehead. Hold tightly, then release and relax.

Stop all activity for a few moments, and notice how it feels to have all your muscles freed of tension. Become aware of your body as a whole. Feel yourself held down by the earth's gravitational pull.

Feel the gratitude for this awareness within your body.

## CLEARING THE STAGE

One of the best images to help us embrace silence of the mind and awareness comes from leadership coach David Rock, author of *Your Brain at Work*. He invites us to take a few minutes each day to sit in silence, using the image of a small theatrical stage:[9]

Think of this stage as your working memory (what you are concentrating on at the moment). When thoughts go through your mind, it is as if they are actors taking the stage. Gently clear the stage and sit in silence. As thoughts interfere, gently direct the thoughts—the actors—off the stage. You can do this for a few minutes at a time and build up to more time.

Clearing the mind is the essence of silent meditation. People who are less visual may prefer listening to their breath, and other people prefer a sacred word or phrase to help with concentration. It doesn't matter how you clear the stage; it matters that you do it. And it helps to do it regularly, even if you feel like you don't do it very well. The benefit comes from the sweeping of the stage rather than keeping the stage totally clear.

Clearing the stage allows the analytical part of your brain, the prefrontal cortex, to take a break. From this pause, says Rock, insight and wisdom can come forward. As we clear the stage of our minds, we can focus on the presence of God, and being in that presence is the simplest and most sincere prayer we can offer. We want nothing from God but to be in God's presence.

## "HERE I AM" PRAYER

The "Here I am" prayer is a simple three-step prayer adapted from Russian Orthodox bishop Anthony Bloom's classic *Beginning to Pray*.[10] It's another way to clear the stage or to drop into sacred silence.

Set aside at least five minutes. Do not answer the phone or allow yourself to be distracted from your goal. Be seated and say to yourself, "Here I am, seated, doing nothing. I will do nothing for five minutes" (or longer, depending on the time you set for yourself).

1. First, notice what is around you. Say to yourself, "Here I am, present to this room (garden, chapel, wherever you are)." Be aware of the furniture, walls, and any pets or people in the room. Just be present and silent in your environment. Relax deeply.

2. Notice your body, mind, and spirit. Relax your body. Allow your thoughts to float by without stopping to ruminate on any one of them. Let your spirit be free. Notice what you feel inside. Say to yourself, "Here I am, present to myself."

3. As your body, mind, and spirit settle down, say to yourself, "Here I am, present to God." Repeat silently to God, "Here I am." Bask in the presence of the Holy until you have prayed for your allotted time.

## BEFRIENDING SILENCE

Part of our journey requires that we slow down and allow time for the Holy Spirit to work in us. Becoming comfortable in silence—simply being present in the moment—may take some practice, but it will enhance the journey considerably.

In Quaker worship, people sit in silence with no goal or motive other than to be ready to hear what the Spirit says to them. When worshippers experience what they call a "leading from God," they may share it. Sometimes they experience no particular leading. Sometimes they are given a word, phrase, deep feeling, or image. Occasionally, someone will begin to sing. But silence is the prayer.

Set aside a time for silent prayer. This means more than just not speaking out loud. It means relinquishing words and stilling your mind. Open yourself to whatever the Spirit may want to say to you or move you to do. Dismiss any preconceived notions about what "should" happen and just be in the presence of God. Do not judge yourself. You may or may not experience a leading from God while you are silent. Rest in *just being*. But if you do experience a leading, allow yourself to enjoy and appreciate it! Sit in gratitude for whatever you receive.

## CENTERING PRAYER

Centering prayer is a popular Christian contemplative practice mentioned earlier in this chapter. In this prayer, you don't seek a word or leading from God. You seek only the mystery we call God.

Centering prayer has just one guideline: you choose a sacred word to return to whenever your mind wanders. If you have trouble coming up with a word, consider using the word *hope, joy, peace*, or *serenity*.

> Sit in a sturdy chair with your feet flat on the ground, and dedicate yourself to being still inwardly as well as physically. If you begin to ruminate, worry, or find your mind wandering instead of being in silence, bring your attention back to your sacred word. That's all there is to it.

Many people find centering prayer difficult at first, but don't be discouraged! Although the human mind evolved to be active and alert, we can practice centering prayer and discover that—over time—we enter into contemplation (deep awareness of God's presence).

Use your sacred word to return to silence as many times as you need to. Try beginning with ten minutes of centering prayer, and work up to twenty minutes.

## JESUS PRAYER

In the Gospel of Mark, Bartimaeus cries out to Jesus, "Son of David, have mercy on me" (Mark 10:47). Orthodox Christians in the Middle Ages used this cry as a repetitive, sacred prayer. They find the name of Jesus is a source of power and grace, leading to a state of inner silence they called *hesychia*.

Choose a variation of the Jesus Prayer that you feel most comfortable with:

- Lord Jesus Christ, Son of God, have mercy on me, a sinner.

- Jesus Christ, have mercy on me.

- Jesus, have mercy.

- Lord, have mercy.

- Mercy.

You may offer this prayer in a comfortable seated position, or you may choose to walk around while praying.

Breathe naturally, and repeat the Jesus Prayer silently for the length of time you have chosen.

When distractions crop up, return to the prayer.

## PRAYER OF THE HEART

You may choose your own contemplative prayer mantra. By spending a few minutes locating your deep longing and your favorite name for God, you can create your "prayer of the heart." Here's how:

Begin seated in a comfortable position. Take a few deep, slow breaths, and allow the tension of the day to flow out with each exhalation. Then allow your breath to find its natural pace.

What is your deepest and truest desire in this moment? If

you find your desires feel "tacky" or too worldly, try suspending judgment and instead looking at what's at the base of that desire. When you check in with your deepest and truest self, what is it that you want from God?

When you identify your deepest desire, name it with a short phrase. For example, if your deep desire is inner freedom, then your phrase would be "freedom" or "inner freedom." Make sure your desire phrase is not too long.

Then ask what your favorite name for God is. How do you image the Creator? Choose whatever name seems to fit best for you. Some examples include Jesus, Higher Power, Wisdom, Father, Mother, or Mystery. Be as creative as you want to be. But again, keep the name rather short.

Combine your name for God with your desire. For example, if your phrase is "freedom" and the name you choose for God is Christ, your prayer of the heart might be "Freedom, in Christ." Spend a few moments coming up with your two-part prayer.

Begin to say—either aloud or silently—your phrase. You may inhale on the name for God and exhale on the desire, or vice versa. Spend several minutes breathing this prayer. Make it your own. Allow God to inhabit this prayer.

After several minutes of repeating this prayer, sink into contemplative silence. Allow the love of God to fill you and surround you.

If you want to recall this phrase throughout the day, write it down. You might want to place it on the back of a business card and put it in your wallet or pocket. Or place a note next to your computer or on the door of your refrigerator.

## EVALUATING OUR READINESS

Assessing progress along a spiritual path is tricky. The journey is not a test we have to score high on, *or else*. God grants us grace, so we need to grant grace to ourselves. The following checklist can and should be used by individuals; however, our focus in each chapter's section on evaluation will be on congregational growth.

One of the best ways to evaluate a congregation's readiness for a journey that deepens their relationship with God and building spiritual vitality is to notice how members talk about their faith. Are they ready and willing to talk about how God has shown up in their lives? If not, keep encouraging people to practice the awareness exercises, and offer times for individuals to share their faith stories. Only a few people need to open up before others become more comfortable. When people realize that we all have experiences of God and that these aren't all burning bushes or walks on water, they are more likely to share how God is active in their daily lives.

Learning how others experience God can help us recognize our own experience and think more broadly about what an experience of God is like. We may not have the momentous aha experience that Thomas Merton had on that Louisville street corner. But one day we may sense a deep word of encouragement in our heart or a peace that "passes all understanding" in silent prayer.

Let's allow God to approach us in a way that resonates with us.

One of the ways to help us name such threads of connection in the practice of awareness is to answer several important questions together. Here is a checklist that may help as you and your congregation spend time with the prep exercises and seek to be more aware of God, while discerning what is important in your communal life. Spend time getting to the heart of these questions, for your shared answers may reveal significant wisdom for your next steps on the road ahead.

You might ask any of these questions:

- Do we feel closer to God?

- Do we have a deeper understanding of our connection to God?

- As we listen to others share their experience of God, do we sense a resonance with our own experience?

- Is our heart inclining more toward love these days?

- Are we experiencing a flow of energy to and for others?

- Are we able to relax and be in the present moment more often?

- Do we feel increasing freedom to be who we were created to be?

- Are we following Jesus more out of a sense of joy and freedom than a sense of obligation and duty?

- Are we developing a deeper understanding of our gifts and how they might be best used in the world?

- What are we learning about ourselves and God as we come into greater awareness of the world and God's presence all around us?

- And the final and most important way to evaluate where we are with God: How is the "fruit of the Spirit" (love, joy, peace, gentleness, goodness, faith, meekness, temperance; see Gal 5:22) evident in our life?

## CONCLUSION

We hope you have enjoyed getting on the road! The next stop is reflecting on what we notice from our increased awareness of God.

# Spiritual Reflection

I remember the days of old;
   I think about all your deeds;
   I meditate on the work of your hands.
—Psalm 143:5

Becoming aware of God's presence in our lives and in the world is a crucial step in our spiritual transformation. It solidifies our faith and inspires us along the way. For most of us, the moments of acute awareness of the Spirit's movement in our lives are special and occasional. Old-timers called these "mountaintop experiences," and we don't get to the mountaintop every day. But once we've been there, it's helpful to practice remembering those special moments of deep connection and to ponder how they have changed our lives and how we can continue to be transformed by the insight gleaned from these important moments.

Paying attention to what is holy and being grateful for those moments is countercultural and always has been. Remember the story of Jesus healing ten lepers and only one remembering and turning back to thank Jesus and praise God (Luke 17:11–19)? The world moves very fast, and we, like those nine lepers who failed to stop and show gratitude, become impatient to get on with our lives. When we slow down, we may find ourselves out of step with our "moving at the speed of life" culture. But if we simply take all these wonderful gifts without spending time appreciating them, then we are missing out on the fullness of the blessing.

Spiritual reflection is the intentional focus on how God is trying to communicate with us. Much as Elijah contemplated the fire, earthquake, and wind, wondering whether God was speaking to him through them, we also wonder about God's voice and presence in our lives. We seek to discern God's work among us—a practice for which we have biblical guidelines but few absolute commandments. For example, if a voice tells us to kill someone or to steal, we know the commandments that prohibit those choices. Voices and leadings from God on matters for which there are many *good* choices are more difficult to discern, and we do well to check those out in consultation with our faith community, Scripture, historical tradition, personal experience, and reason. We discuss ways to test a "leading" you believe to be from God later in this chapter (page 46), and we will address discernment in more detail in chapter 3.

In Elijah's case, God spoke out of "a sound of sheer silence" (1 Kgs 19:12). Many people find that spiritual reflection opens them to this kind of holy silence, and others find practices such as dialogue, writing, creating art, or walking more helpful in connecting with God. We offer a variety of practices in our Congregational Spiritual Road Map for this chapter, in the hope that you will find a few that work well for your congregation.

Spiritual reflection is also remembering God's presence throughout history. Mystic and rabbi Baal Shem Tov (1698–1760) is quoted as saying, "Forgetfulness leads to exile, while remembrance is the secret of redemption."[1] We remember God's presence in our lives, so we can pass that knowledge on to others now and in the future, enabling faith not only to survive but to grow. The story of the people of Israel's escape from Egypt includes Moses's plea, "Remember this day on which you came out of Egypt, out of the house of slavery, because the Lord brought you out from there by strength of hand" (Exod 13:3). Ancient Christian liturgies for the Eucharist include a prayer of remembrance, reviewing important events in the life of the people of Israel and also in the life of Jesus and the birth of the church. Why recite these? As Elizabeth Liebert, emerita professor of spiritual life at San Francisco Theological Seminary, says, "The way to the future sometimes comes to us from the past."[2] It reminds us we are part of a history that God has been working in all along.

For congregations, this type of reflection may involve reconstructing a history of events that shaped the life of the church. This history also recalls events in the church and the wider world and especially the congregation's responses then and now, and it includes how the Spirit is speaking to the congregation through the events. One of the first spiritual directors to work specifically with institutions, Christian brother John H. Mostyn, recommends researching as far back as the story of the founding of your organization: "Usually the story of the founding most clearly shows the authenticity of the spirit vision at work. Once the present-day inhabitants of the institution hear the story, the opportunity is created for them to embrace the founding spirit and/or let the spirit vision embrace them. They can then begin to tell the difference between what is helpful in the institution today and what is not."[3] That "founding spirit" information shows what has been helpful over time, and it is not only inspirational, but it also becomes critical information to any discernment process a group might undertake.

## SPIRITUAL REFLECTION IN ACTION

One church that Teresa worked with spent considerable time reflecting on its historical timeline and noticed that, throughout its hundred-plus years, it had birthed a number of other congregations and nonprofits. In viewing the timeline and noticing this, the congregation realized, "We're an incubator!" This aha moment led them to ask themselves and God, "What is being born in us now, even as our congregation is getting older and less energetic?"

Chad's work in middle judicatory ministry brings him in contact with congregations during times of deep spiritual reflection. In one case, Chad was working with a congregation that didn't feel they were being called to close but had already decided to sell their building. While they spent time reflecting on where God was leading, a profound sense of grief surfaced. This congregation had been in the community since the late nineteenth century in one form or another and had at one point merged with two nearby churches. The building was in a trendy part of town with significant opportunities for ministry all around. The idea that the church was going to sell its building, after all it had been through, was distressing.

Chad invited the group to enter into a practice called *lectio divina* (found in this chapter's Congregational Spiritual Road Map), using the first two verses of Psalm 46:

God is our refuge and strength
    a very present help in trouble.
Therefore, we will not fear, though the earth should change,
    though the mountains shake in the heart of the sea.

In this prayer, the group was drawn to the words *refuge*, *fear*, *change*, and *strength*. The awareness of their grief and God's presence in the midst of the unknown led them into even deeper

42

reflection around times they needed refuge, felt fear, or were forced to change and how they found the strength needed for that journey. Specifically, they recalled the time the church building had caught fire. One woman shared her experience of standing in the sanctuary after the fire and seeing that the only thing in the building still intact and not covered with soot or ash was the stained-glass window of Jesus praying in the Garden of Gethsemane. "It was as if Jesus was in the pain with us in that moment."

Chad asked, "What is Jesus saying to you right now?" She replied, "I am with you in the pain of saying good-bye to this sacred space, that I am your refuge and strength, that through all the change and though the mountains should shake, I will be there."

The sacred work of reflection offers us opportunities to dig deeper into our experience, painful though it may be. It offers our communities the chance to see things more clearly and begin to put together a larger picture of what God might be saying to us.

## THE GIFTS OF CONSOLATION AND DESOLATION

Our goal in this stage of the journey is remembering holy consolation—appreciating the joy and experiencing anew the gratitude we have for our relationship with God. It's also helpful to reflect on our "valley" experiences of disconnectedness from God, known as desolation. Both principles offer opportunities for spiritual growth.

The terms *consolation* and *desolation* to describe our spiritual condition come from the writings of Ignatius of Loyola, cofounder of the Society of Jesus (Jesuits), an order of the Roman Catholic Church, around the time of the Protestant Reformation in the mid-sixteenth century. Ignatius was not particularly religious when, as a young Basque soldier, he was seriously injured in the 1521 Battle of Pamplona. His recovery required a long recuperation in a convent. An avid reader of romance novels, Ignatius craved reading material but had nothing available other than *The Life of Christ* by Ludolph of Saxony, a fourteenth-century Carthusian, and a book entitled *Flowers of the Saints*, stories about Catholic saints. He spent his recovery time reading these religious books as well as fantasizing about being a dashing knight devoted to a lady (a common desire of young men at the time).

Ignatius began to notice that when he had romantic fantasies, he felt passion and excitement for a bit but was ultimately left "dry and dusty," to use his language. He also noticed that when he read about Jesus or the saints, especially Francis of Assisi, he felt a deep and lasting desire to be like them. These insights led him to write about two important movements of the heart: *consolation*, a pull or movement toward God, and *desolation*, a push away from God. He felt consolation when reading about the saints and desolation when daydreaming about romance. And he decided he wanted to follow the way of consolation.

Lots of people speak of consolation as the feeling of being comforted and supported.[4] Ignatius uses the word in a much broader sense, referring to deep emotion—which he calls movements of the heart—that draws us closer to God. It can also refer to a sense of God being with us through events in life. If you have ever felt in sync with the Holy Spirit, filled with joy, hope, love, lasting peace, energy, life, or comfort, you have experienced consolation. But consolation is not something we experience only when life seems good. We can find ourselves comforted and held by God even in times of deep grief and sadness. When looking for consolation, it helps to consider moments when something holy, awesome, or mysterious breaks through and touches our heart.

Desolation is the other side of the emotional coin. It's more than feeling down and out, which is how we use the term in casual conversation. Ignatius uses desolation to refer to any movement of the heart that draws us away from the goodness of God. For him, desolation occurs when we turn away from God or get caught up in a whirlwind of negative emotion, such as uncontrolled anger, restlessness, anxiety, chaos, apathy, lethargy, or coldheartedness.[5] Desolation may not be desirable, but it is helpful. Think of it as more of a warning sign or a teachable moment than as a failing or sin. For example, if we take a path in life that seems inspired by God but find ourselves in constant desolation, it's time to stop and reflect on the wisdom of our choice.

Both consolation and desolation are to be expected in life, and the process of becoming aware of them and learning from them helps us mature in faith. We suggest congregational leaders take ample time to discuss and practice naming consolation and desolation, so people in your congregation are able to articulate when they do (and do not) feel the presence of God both in their personal life and in the life of their congregation.

The best way to do this is to have individuals in your congregation use the Ignatian Examen (found in this chapter's Congregational Spiritual Road Map) daily for a month or so, and then gather to discuss moments in which they experienced consolation and desolation. We'll share even more about the examen in chapter 3, because it figures prominently in the practice of discernment.

## SAVORING AND ACCEPTING

Once we've named consolation, savoring is the simple spiritual practice of taking time to enjoy it—to remember moments when we felt deeply connected to God and allow ourselves to feel that connection again. Savoring is basking in gratitude for God's blessings and then asking, "OK, God, now what?" What does this gratitude lead us to do or be in the world?

Recalling the past can also bring up harsh memories, actions, and attitudes within ourselves or our congregations that we'd rather not look at. It wasn't easy for the church Chad was working with to remember the pain of the fire. But that's where they could find the insight about God's presence in their grief. Growing spiritually requires acceptance of the very emotions we prefer to resist—usually fear, sadness, anger, anxiety, and frustration. It requires recognition that if God is in all things, God must be in our pain. Accepting our difficult emotions, just as they are, and again, exploring the question we ask while savoring—"OK, God, now what?"—can provide valuable insights for our spiritual path.

## REFLECTION ON THE MOVEMENT OF THE SPIRIT

With all this talk of spiritual reflection and listening to God, you may be thinking, "How do we know it's God we are experiencing, not just our ego or imagination? How do we know when God's Spirit is moving, leading, or encouraging us?" We have good reason to be cautious about saying we hear God's voice, because we've seen examples of people claiming to be acting on God's behalf while doing ungodly things! The writer of 1 John says, "Beloved, do not believe every spirit, but test the spirits to see whether they are from God: for many false prophets have gone out into the world" (4:1).

We can test what we believe are messages from God by determining if they are in line with Jesus's Great Commandments: love God and love your neighbor as yourself (Matt 22:37–38). We also test messages to see if they are in line with what we know about God from Scripture. For example, here are some helpful Scripture passages for identifying what is mostly likely "of God":

- **The nature of Wisdom (Wis 7:22—8:1).** Wisdom, in biblical wisdom literature, is personified as a woman and described as holy, clear, humane, steadfast, free from anxiety, penetrating through all spirits.

- **Beatitudes (Matt 5–7).** The Sermon on the Mount (or Luke's Sermon on the Plain) includes excellent benchmarks for discerning the Spirit's movement in our lives. Is our choice merciful? Does it come from a pure heart? Is it just? Does it contribute to peace?

- **Fruit of the Spirit (Gal 5:22).** Jesus frequently taught that we can know what is holy by its "fruit." Paul named the fruits of love, joy, peace, gentleness, goodness, faith, meekness, and temperance.

- **Think on these things (Phil 4:8–9).** This list is designed to help Christians stay focused on God. It's also a good guide for testing the spirits: "Whatever is true, honorable, just, pure, pleasing, commendable, any excellence, anything worthy of praise—think about these things."

- **Wisdom from above (Jas 3:17–18).** God's wisdom is pure, peaceable, gentle, willing to yield, full of mercy and good fruits, without a trace of partiality or hypocrisy. Is what we are experiencing of God? If it fulfills the Wisdom test, we can trust that it probably is.

These scripture passages are the most reliable way we know of determining whether a movement of the heart is from God. They can help you determine where you are experiencing consolation and, by contrast, desolation. They are excellent benchmarks for your spiritual reflection.

## CONGREGATIONAL SPIRITUAL ROAD MAP: PRACTICES FOR REFLECTION

Your congregation may already be familiar with many of the following practices. Use ones that feel like a good fit for your journey. We recommend adding new ones to the exercises people are familiar with because using new ones may draw in people who have not yet found a prayer practice that connects them to God in a profound way.

We begin this part of the journey with a simple exercise reflecting on freedom.

### FREEDOM REFLECTION

It is amazing how the presence of God fills the room as people tell stories of moments when they felt freedom. Paul wrote to the Galatians, "For freedom Christ has set us free" (Gal 5:1), so we can trust that God's desire for us is freedom—not the cheap kind of freedom that might lead us to abandon responsibilities and run away, but the kind of freedom that allows us to feel fully alive as we follow Christ out of love and gratitude rather than obligation.

For this exercise, begin by asking individuals to recall a time in their lives when they felt completely and totally free—free in mind, body, and spirit.

Relive that moment. Feel it in your body. What were you doing? Who were you with? What was the setting? What preceded the feeling of freedom? What did the feeling of freedom lead to?

48

Sit in silence with the memory. Invite the Holy Spirit to speak to you through this memory.

After a good bit of silence (at least five minutes), invite people to share their moments of freedom and what that freedom feels like now. What did they notice about reflecting on freedom? Does a theme emerge as people share?

Also ask, "When does this congregation experience freedom?" or, "What aspect of congregational life feels most alive and free to us?"

Doing this exercise helps congregations notice when and where they experience true freedom so that out of that awareness, they can make choices that lead to even more freedom.

## THE EXAMEN

The prayer of examen comes from Ignatius, whose motto was "finding God in all things," which means reflecting on all things and considering how God is showing up—in both the pleasant and unpleasant experiences. The practice he handed down is simple and helpful for individuals, small groups, and congregations. It can be adapted in a variety of ways, so experiment with what you think would work best for you or your congregation. Here is a script you can use as a guide to lead the prayer.[6]

Begin by opening yourself to God's grace and love, asking for God to be revealed to you in this prayer.

Ponder a specific period of time in your congregation's life—perhaps a day, week, month, or year or an event.

In that period, when did you feel most deeply connected to God? If that question doesn't work well for you, consider when you felt most alive or filled with peace. Allow plenty of time in silence to return to that moment and savor it.

In that period, when did you feel most disconnected from God? You may also ask yourself when you felt least alive or when your peace was most disturbed. Allow yourself to feel that moment again and accept it without judgment.

Now ask God's Spirit to offer whatever you need in this moment. Be still, and allow God-space to reveal whatever you need to learn from this practice. Notice if any insight, image, or feeling comes to you. It's OK if nothing comes to mind. Don't force it, and don't berate yourself (or God!) if nothing happens in that silence.

In gratitude, be still and allow God to be present to you in silence.

Once finished with the examen, you may write in a journal, talk with a prayer partner, or if you are doing this in a group, discuss what each of you noticed.

Congregations, church boards, or worship committees can use the examen regularly to get a feel for which events, activities, or worship elements are drawing members closer to God and which are not.

## MEDITATE ON THE WORK OF GOD'S HANDS

Lead a discussion in your church about what moves people's hearts. We can become so wrapped up in the tasks of daily life and the pressures to produce that we forget to take in the beauty of creation. Our religious communities may become so focused on bringing about change in the world that we fail to appreciate the splendor right in front of us. Or we may discount the necessity for beauty and harmony.

Ask one or more of the following questions. Take some silence between each person's sharing, and notice how the atmosphere changes.

- Where is the most beautiful place you have ever been?

- What sight melts your heart?

- What makes you stop and take notice?

- What, in this material world, lifts you into transcendence?

## REFLECT ON YOUR CONGREGATION'S HISTORY

This is a common exercise churches use in preparation for strategic planning or mission statement revision. It requires butcher paper, colored markers, heavy tape, and at least three hours of time. You should invite a number of members who've been with the church for many years to be on hand. They will remember events and situations that were important to the life of the congregation. Also, have members dig up any old church memorabilia, such as written histories, photos, or letters.

When introducing this exercise, emphasize the importance of remembering both the good and bad times. Everything matters in this timeline.

Hang a long piece of butcher paper along a wall for all to see. You may want to double the paper in case the markers bleed through.

Draw a horizontal line across the length of the paper in the middle.

Mark the birth of the church or organization at the left end and the present at the right end. Place marks between them to indicate decades or years (depending on how old your church is).

With your group, begin making notes on the timeline of the following events:

- Changes in pastoral, music and other key staff

- Deaths of important members or staff

- Changes in or additions to the building, including any capital campaigns

- Dates when significant programs began and/or ended

- Important (positive or negative) events in the life of the church

- Changes in the neighborhood around the church that affected the congregation

- Events in the wider community, state, nation, or world that had significant effects on the church

Take some silence, and ask the group to look at the timeline. If someone sees that something is missing, invite them to quietly add it to the timeline.

The heart of the timeline practice is the discussion it generates. Ask, "What do you notice about the history of this church? Are there patterns this church repeats? What has gotten this church into trouble? Has our mission changed since the church was founded? Is there something we need to return to? Is there something we need to let go of? Who is represented in the time-line? Who is left out?"

Close by asking God to use this timeline to reveal important information to the congregation for its discernment.

Leave the timeline up for several weeks, and let everyone at the church take a look at it.

## SAVORING GOD'S PRESENCE

One of the best ways to appreciate God's presence is to reflect on the list of the "fruit of the Spirit" from the list in Galatians 5:22. Choose a "fruit of the Spirit" you want the congregation to focus on. Ask, "When in our life together did we feel an over-whelming sense of this fruit?"

Invite individuals in the group to return in silence to that moment and to relive it. Ask them to remember as much as they can about it. Probe for details as needed with these questions:

• Who were you with?

• What were you doing?

• What did the surroundings look like?

• What do you feel (emotionally and physically) as you recall this moment?

The goal is to stay with this memory and allow it to have new life. Watch, listen, and simply be open to God's presence again in the memory.

After a sufficient time of reflection, close the prayer, and invite people to share their memory and where that memory led them in the prayer. Allow plenty of time for silence before and after each person's reflections. Most groups become deeply quiet and moved during this prayer, so don't rush.

## WHERE DO WE SEE GOD?

A powerful community practice is to name as many attributes of God as possible and then ponder when and where we notice those attributes in community's life. Also consider when and where we notice the *lack* of those attributes. As a guide, use the attributes found in the Scripture passages listed on page 47.

### *Lectio Divina,* or Sacred Reading

As illustrated by Chad's story about the church selling its building, praying with Scripture is a powerful way of opening ourselves to the presence of God. For this prayer, we set aside our need to know the history, context, or other facts about the passage. Instead, we ask the Spirit to speak to us in a word, phrase, or image from the passage that relates to our spiritual path. It's important to choose a short piece of Scripture (or even a poem or passage of prose) and to allow plenty of time for this five-step prayer. For some people, journaling during this prayer will be helpful. Here's a template you can use in leading this prayer with a group:

Step 1: *Silencio.* Keeping your chosen text nearby, invite the people who are gathered to become still and quiet within, silently turning all thoughts and desires over to God. This is a time to let go of concerns, worries, or agendas and just be present for a few moments.

**Step 2:** *Lectio.* Explain to the group that you will read a short passage aloud slowly two or three times, with a period of silence between each reading. Ask them to notice any word, phrase, or image that seems to have energy for them. It could be a word that invites, a phrase that puzzles, or an image that intrigues. Encourage them to allow this word, phrase, or image to choose them. If they are journaling, they could write down what comes to mind.

**Step 3:** *Meditatio.* Invite your group to take whatever word, phrase, or image from your Scripture passage that has energy for them and ponder it in their hearts. In this phase, we ruminate over what stands out for us. Invite them to allow this word, phrase, or image to speak to them at their deepest level—amid thoughts, desires, memories. How does it connect with their lives?

**Step 4:** *Oratio.* In this step, we ask God to transform us by the word, phrase, or image we have been meditating on. This is a time to allow our hearts to be in dialogue with God. Invite participants to reflect on how this word, phrase, or image connects with their life today. How is God present in it? This is another good step to journal with.

**Step 5:** *Contemplatio.* The final step is to put away journals, pens, thoughts, and images, and to sink silently into the presence of God (taking about five minutes). After the silence, allow some time for people in the group to share their word, phrase, or image and its connection to their life. Allow plenty of time for people to share before drawing the prayer to a close.

If you would like a simpler version of *lectio divina*, try this:

Choose a Scripture passage. Let the group know you will read it two or three times, with silence between each reading. As they hear the Scripture, they are to notice any words, phrases, or images that capture their imagination or seem to have energy for them.

Read the short passage two or three times slowly.

Pause and invite the group to sit silently with the word, phrase, or image that resonated with them.

Ask them to remain in silence and notice how that word, phrase, or image relates to their life today. Is there something to learn from it? An insight? A challenge?

Take a bit more silence to allow them to open to any insight God may have for them.

Ask the group to share any insights from this prayer they feel comfortable sharing.

Thank God for any insight or new awareness of God received from the lectio.

## WALK A LABYRINTH

For those who pray best when they are in motion, the labyrinth is a wonderful tool. A labyrinth is an ancient symbol, usually circular, that includes a path you follow to the center, where you stop and pray, and then you walk the same path back out. It is symbolic of the spiritual path toward God (represented by the space at the center). The classic use of the labyrinth is divided into three stages:

1. **Purgation.** As you walk toward the center, you let go of all that keeps you from God.

2. **Illumination.** As you enter the center, you sit or stand in silent prayer, resting in God's presence and allowing the Spirit to enlighten you.

3. **Union.** As you walk away from the center, one with God, you carry this light into the world, opening yourself to the world in service to God.

You can be creative in how you walk a labyrinth. You may use the walking meditation to remember an experience you want to savor, to pray for something important, and as a way of mulling over a discernment question. Most people walk the path at a relaxed pace, allowing themselves to calm down. The key element is that as you walk, you open yourself to the fullness of God's Spirit in your life and heart.

Walking a labyrinth has become such a popular spiritual practice that you can find labyrinths on the grounds of many churches. If you have no labyrinth nearby, create a similar experience for yourself by mapping a circular route for walking outdoors. Consider the first half of the circle to be the "way in" and then stop at the midpoint for silence and rest in God. Finally, complete the circle as your "way out." You can even map a winding route through a neighborhood. Or if the building where you worship is large, with many rooms and passageways, you can lay out a labyrinth-style path leading to and away from a center prayer room.

## VISUAL PRAYER

Another way to remember experiences of God is to create a visual representation. You don't have to be an artist to pray in this way, nor does your representation have to be recognizable to anyone but you. Many people find that drawing, painting, or even doodling while in prayer helps them discover new aspects of their relationship with God. If you have a question for discernment, you can explore that in this process. Your visual representation may offer some clues for you that will help you make your choice. Or there may be some deep sadness or desolation you need to express.

If drawing or painting is not your choice, you can create a collage or other visual art that reflects what you are feeling in prayer. Choosing photos, clippings, and other objects, arranging them on paper, and gluing them down as a representation can be a contemplative practice. The same is true for molding clay or making art from fabric and fibers.

Here's a suggested format for doing visual prayer:

Begin with a question or statement of intention. Write it on your art paper or an index card, and keep it close by.

Create your visual art as you hold that question or intention in prayer. Allow plenty of time for the art to be created.

Sharing each individual work of art in a group provides a window into each person's inner world and can help group members notice common threads and themes.

## FOCUSING

Focusing teaches us to listen to the wisdom of the body—not just the mind, but the whole of our being. The practice of focusing was created by philosophy professor Eugene Gendlin.[7] It was later adapted as a practice of "bio-spirituality" by Edwin McMahon and Peter Campbell.[8] The focusing prayer is based on a biophysical method for listening to hurting places (emotional, spiritual, and physical) within our bodies.[9] The prayer involves creative visualization and imagination, so when leading it, prepare your group for something that might feel different to them. Allow at least twenty minutes for this practice. Give the instructions slowly, allowing time for the felt senses and insights to emerge.

Here's an outline you can follow when leading this prayer:

Explain that this is a body prayer that uses imagination and felt senses—physical as well as emotional. Tell participants you will ask them to silently respond to a series of questions. They may write down their responses, but if writing feels like a distraction, there is no need to interrupt the exercise to write.

Guide participants as follows:

• Ask God to be present to you in your body and your "felt senses."

• Close your eyes and slow your breathing. Let your awareness settle to the center of your body. What do you feel there?

• What location or part of your body wants your awareness right now? (Spend time allowing this to emerge.) Is there an important feeling in your body that needs attention right now?

• Communicate with this felt sense in your body. Silently tell it, "I'm here. I'm listening." Ask this bodily feeling if it's all right to go further.

• Try to describe this felt sense or sensation in your body. Is there an image that emerges? If it helps, give it a name (such as "tight neck" or "lump in the throat").

• Sit with this body awareness without judgment. Simply observe.

• Does this bodily sense have an emotional quality? If so, what is it?

• Ask, "What causes the emotion?

• Ask the sensation what it needs.

• Ask your body to show you how healing would feel.

• You may want to put your hand on that part of the body and send it warmth. Also, you may want to ask Jesus, God, or the Holy Spirit to help you care for this part of yourself.

• Gently end your conversation with the felt sense. Thank your body and its senses for being with you in this prayer.

Invite conversation about what happened for people in this prayer. Where did they feel God's healing touch most deeply? How is it to pray in this way? How is it to listen to their body?

Close with a spoken prayer thanking God for being present in this prayer.

## EVALUATING OUR GROWTH IN REFLECTION

Here are some questions to ask after a period of reflection within your congregation, beginning with the most important question about spiritual growth:

• Are we feeling more life and energy as a result of the practices, changes, and/or sense of call we have named? Where does our congregation feel vibrant and alive? Where does it feel dull? (Doing the prayer of examen over a long period of time and looking at the progress—or lack of it—toward vitality can be your all-purpose tool for evaluating spiritual growth.)

- Has our time of reflection led us to feel closer to God? If so, how? If not, what was in the way?

- How was it to reflect on our organization's history? Did we notice themes? Have we stayed true to the founder's mission? Did the mission change?

- Are we ready to move on from awareness and reflection to discernment?

If the participants are ready, read on. If not, consider what part of the journey you may need to revisit before moving forward.

# Discernment

The word is very near to you. It is in your mouth and in your heart for you to observe.
—Deuteronomy 30:14

Congregations face hard decisions. They must discern the mission and vision of the church, pastoral staffing needs, ways to care for their building, and whether to continue historic ministries or to begin new ones—just to name a few of the decisions they commonly make. In some cases, a congregation will reach a place where they must decide whether they will become a legacy church and close with dignity or take steps to revitalize their ministry for their future.

The challenge is to ask what God is inviting your congregation to be or do at any given time—and to listen to what God is saying. The good news is that you probably are already doing this, at least in part:

- If your congregation has ever prayed for guidance while making an important choice, you've done discernment.

- If your community has ever listened to a collective gut feeling and gone with that, you've done discernment.

- Or if you've waited patiently for the right time to take a next step, that's discernment.

- If your congregation has ever made a list of the pros and cons of various options and then used that list to help decide which path to pursue, you've done discernment.

- All those times you've imagined the kind of church God was calling you to become, you were participating in the spiritual practice of discernment.

Although you already know quite a bit about discernment, some of what you think you know may be wrong. In some cases, discernment has developed a bad reputation. Here's what it is not:

- **A synonym for an authoritarian decision-making process.** Perhaps a small group of people at church got their way by bullying but called it discernment. It's not a practice we do so we can hold our decision over others, saying, "God told us to do this, so you had better butt out!" Humility and an openness to whatever God shows us in the process are essential.

- **A stalling tactic.** You may have heard of a group using discernment to delay making any decision at all and concluded that applying principles of discernment to your choices will just take too long.

- **A process used only by clergy or those feeling called to professional ministry.** Yes, the term *discern-*

*ment* is used in religious circles to refer to any number of processes people go through to become ordained, join an order, or receive a commission to do a special kind of ministry. Some of those processes are discernment, and some are attempts at gatekeeping (which is important but not necessarily discernment).

In this chapter, we will give you a more detailed and complete picture of the Christian spiritual practice of discernment, one that combines wisdom from a number of sources.

## WHAT IS DISCERNMENT?

Discernment is the practice of noticing where God's spirit is alive in us, then sifting and sorting through all of what we notice—the information, feelings, insights, intuition, beliefs, and values—so that we can make a faithful choice. It's about paying attention to God's leading, but it's not about "finding God's perfect will so we will be super successful," nor is it a special formula that inoculates against mistakes. You can use all the processes and prayer practices in this book and end up with a decision that doesn't work out the way you wanted. In our experience, though, congregations doing intentional discernment are far more likely to have a satisfactory outcome than those that fly by the seat of their pants. And even if your outcome seems less than favorable to you at the outset, don't despair. You may need to do more discernment, or maybe you just need to wait to see progress.

Of course, prayer is essential to discernment, but as mentioned earlier, discernment also includes other efforts:

- **Paying attention to "felt senses" in your body.** What if you pray about a path and feel it is the right one, but deep in the pit of your stomach, something tells you to wait? The principles of Christian spiritual discernment advise you to pay attention to *all* the information you receive about a choice. That includes what you feel in the pit of your stomach. It could be the Spirit telling you more information is needed before you make that decision.

- **Making a list of the pros and cons.** It's helpful to put on paper the many advantages and disadvantages of an option under consideration. When you do this, be sure to consider the weight of each pro and con. Not all your discernment data is equally important.

- **Waiting for clarity on an answer.** Our culture is so fast paced that we sometimes make decisions without taking time to just be with the question.

- **Using your imagination.** Visualizing a possible outcome can be helpful to your process. In the Ignatian process discussed later in this chapter, we'll offer some practices that employ imagination.

While each of these practices is a piece of discernment, each can also lead us astray. That felt sense in your stomach could be heartburn or fear of the change that is being discussed. Your pros-and-cons list could be so long it leads you to frustration or the paralysis of analysis. Your imagination can run away on you. It is possible to become lost in a fantasy. Because we are human and capable of deceiving ourselves, we shouldn't rely on just *one* of these tools; rather, use them all for a balance of mind, body, and spirit in discernment.

## THE WHY OF DISCERNMENT

The *ultimate* goal of Christian spiritual discernment is to live in a way that draws us closer to God. That's the most important why. However, there are many secondary goals as well. We enter discernment because we are constantly faced with options for service, all of which might seem good and even feel urgent. Churches can get caught in the grip of trying to do too much good instead of stopping and asking, "What is *ours* to do in the world?" (Hint: We are not called to salvation by exhaustion.)

Discernment asks, "Where is God leading us in this particular situation?" Because going where God leads is the ultimate mission of a congregation. If the way forward in a situation is simple and everyone agrees to it, we don't need to do a lot of discernment. But that's rarely the case with congregations (or individuals).

Another reason we enter into discernment is to enhance congregational vitality. Congregations that focus on what God is calling them to do not only draw closer to God, but also demonstrate a clarity in their missional ideals and have greater potential for a healthy and vital life. And as Chad points out, congregational vitality is evident in churches of all sizes: There is a yoked parish in southern Indiana made up of two small membership churches in the middle of rural communities. Most churches their size are focused on the "woe is us" mentality, lamenting, "We used to have hundreds of members, and now we are down to twenty-five people. What else can we do?" But these two small Indiana churches don't worry about size. They believe their work is to be the hands and feet of Christ building relationships and partnerships all over the world. They have a clear sense that their work is both local and global. When Hurricane Katrina hit New Orleans, they put together several large trucks full of items needed in the Ninth Ward. They have done work in Kenya and Sri Lanka, just to name a few of the countries where they are connected.

Also, we discern to build community. When you keep an open mind about where God may be leading and begin to discern as a congregation, you cease to be simply a collection of individuals speaking from your experience. You become one body listening for direction from the Holy Spirit. And that's exciting. It's what nurtures and builds our faith.

Discernment is how we grow in faith. The more we use principles of discernment, the more we learn about ourselves and our congregation. Discernment can become how congregations live day to day and not something taken up only when it's time to convene a search committee for a pastor. It's not just for deciding if it's time for a capital campaign or whether we add a band to our music program. It's a way of life.

And finally, we discern together because, as Mary Benet McKinney puts it, "No one can contain all the wisdom of God, for that would be to be God. However, the Spirit desires to share as much of the wisdom as the group can handle at any given time. To do this, different pieces of that wisdom will be given to different folks."[1] As McKinney sees it, group discernment requires the wisdom of all of us, from the sage to the dreamer, the young, the old, and even the one who always plays devil's advocate.

## HISTORY OF DISCERNMENT

Of course, discernment comes from Christian tradition, but is it biblical? Nowhere in Scripture is there a neatly outlined process for discerning God's desire in any given situation. Instead, we have stories that illustrate various elements that make up spiritual discernment.

### MOSES'S CALL AND CONVERSATION WITH GOD (EXODUS 3–4)

God hears the misery of the enslaved people and visits Moses, commanding him to lead the people out of slavery in Egypt. Moses resists God in many ways, and at each turn, God provides what Moses needs—even when Moses begs God to send someone else to do the job. We may not always like what we hear at first when we listen to God, but like Moses, we can stay in conversation with God and trust God to supply what we need to be faithful.

## YOUNG SAMUEL RUNS TO GOD (1 SAM 3–4:1)

Samuel doesn't recognize God's voice but thinks he is hearing his mentor, Eli. When Eli tells him it is the Lord speaking, Samuel listens and begins his life as a prophet. There are times we need help hearing God's voice, and we need a caring and wise guide in discernment. It's one reason discernment is best done in community rather than alone.

## RUTH RESPONDS OUT OF DEEP DESIRE AND LOVE (RUTH 1)

In her grief and out of a deep sense of commitment and love, Ruth clings to her mother-in-law, Naomi, and follows her to a foreign land. This choice leads to a historic outcome. Ruth marries one of Naomi's relatives, Boaz, and they have a child who becomes the grandfather of the future King David. God's call to us does not always involve a struggle. Sometimes, like Ruth, we need only look to our heart's deepest desire.

## NAAMAN THINKS GOD'S WILL SHOULD BE HARDER (2 KGS 5:1–19)

The prophet Elisha tells Naaman, a military commander with a skin disease, to go wash seven times in the River Jordan to be healed. Naaman wants more theatrics or a more difficult task. His servants point out, "If the prophet had commanded you to do something difficult, you would have done it, right?" Naaman sees their point, washes in the river, and is healed. This is another example of how God's invitation to our congregations may be something so simple and easy that we overlook it or dismiss it. The spiritual path isn't always rosy, but it's also not always laid with thorns.

## THE CALL OF THE PROPHETS OF ISRAEL

The biblical-call narratives are popular because we like stories of people overcoming deep challenges to do the right thing. Check any of the prophetic books in the Hebrew Scriptures, and you will find stories fitting this general description:

- God appears unmistakably to the person with a "Thus says the Lord" message for a specific person or nation. The message is frequently a disturbing one that the prophet believes will put him in physical danger. He has to discern, "How do I know this message is from God?"

- The prophet resists sharing the message. Many times, a supernatural event occurs to convince him to obey God. (Think Jonah in the belly of the whale!) This helps the prophet build a case so that when he approaches the powers that be, he can say, "Well, of course this word is from God. Do you think I would be foolish enough to come up with this on my own? It is not I who speaks, but the Lord."

- The prophet reluctantly does what God commands and takes his lumps. He's only recognized as a prophet if what he proclaims comes to pass. So he endures a time of anxiety and waiting.

- The prophet is rarely appreciated because the powers that be resist accepting God's will.

These call stories show us that discernment can be messy and time-consuming. It may take time for a congregational discernment group to accept what they hear in the process and even longer to persuade the larger congregation of their conclusions.

## THE COUNCIL AT JERUSALEM
## AND CIRCUMCISION (ACTS 15:1–35)

One of the best examples of a body of Christians using spiritual discernment in a matter of deep concern to the community is the story of the council at Jerusalem. A serious dispute in the early church emerges over whether Gentiles need to be circumcised in order to be saved. Paul and Barnabas gather the apostles and elders in an assembly to resolve this matter. In that gathering, Peter shares his personal experience of bringing Gentiles to Christ and concludes that we are all saved through the grace of Jesus, regardless of whether we uphold the law of Moses on circumcision. After hearing that, the whole assembly becomes silent.

The next speaker is Paul (who we know previously held strong views about upholding Jewish law), who along with Barnabas testifies about all the "signs and wonders" they have seen God accomplish among the Gentiles. James (considered by many scholars to be the brother of Jesus) appeals to the crowd's understanding of Scripture, citing Amos 9:11–12, which mentions all people seeking the Lord, "even Gentiles over whom my name has been called." James offers a compromise: to eliminate circumcision as an essential practice, "for it has seemed good to the Holy Spirit and to us to impose no further burden" (Acts 15:28).

This story gives us a lot of information about how the elders and apostles of the early church discerned, implying by extension how we should discern, in times of change:

- They took seriously the confusion and hurt that Gentiles were experiencing as some Christians demanded

71

they be circumcised in order to become Christians. Discernment frequently grows out of our "holy discomfort" around a situation that is unfair or difficult.

- They were clear about their question. They came together for discussion around an important and concrete question: Do Gentiles have to be circumcised to be saved?

- They listened to a number of church leaders share their views on the question. Discernment relies on good information from many sources.

- They allowed time for silence so that the Spirit would have room to move and the assembly would have time to calmly assess their choices.

- They consulted Scripture to see what the prophets had to say about inclusion.

- They allowed their minds to be changed. Certainly, some of the elders went into the assembly supporting mandatory circumcision. Nevertheless, they were open to inclusion after more prayer and additional information.

- They sought "what is good to us and to the Holy Spirit" for guidance. The clarity we seek in discernment is the choice that both reflects how the Spirit is leading us and resonates in our hearts.

## LEARNING FROM JESUIT SPIRITUALITY

The practice of Christian spiritual discernment today comes primarily from two Christian traditions for which discernment is a special charism or gift: the Jesuits and the Quakers. Many of the spiritual practices we encourage in this book are traced directly to the contributions of Ignatius of Loyola, who came to understand how the Holy Spirit worked in his life through a series of experiences that he wrote about in his *Spiritual Exercises*.[2] He reflected on his life and noticed important "movements of the heart" and how acting on those movements could draw him closer to God or block him from the closeness that he so desired.

Ignatius taught that we can learn a lot about our spiritual path from our own moments of consolation and desolation. That's why he told his fellow Jesuits they were required to do the Daily Examen (page 49), even if they were too busy to do any other prayer each day. It was that important.

Spending time in prayer, noticing those moments that draw us closer to God and those when we feel somehow blocked, gives us information about how God is speaking to us and where God may be inviting us to change. For discernment, the benefit of the examen comes as we do it over a significant stretch of time and notice patterns and themes.

## JESUITS' PRINCIPLES OF DISCERNMENT

Ignatius was right: the examen is too important for either individuals or faith communities to overlook. The practice, done regularly, shows us patterns of consolation and desolation, offering us invaluable discernment information for choices we need to make in life. Your congregation can practice it by asking and answering the following questions honestly:

- Looking at our options, where do we feel God's presence most deeply?

- And where do we feel an absence of or a block to God's presence?

In discernment, we generally want to move toward consolation and use desolation as an indication that we should be cautious or as an invitation to gather more information.

Another central teaching about discernment that we draw from Ignatius is to let go of any predetermined or preferred outcome regarding our discernment question. This is where most individuals and congregations get stuck in discernment. *Everyone must agree to let go of their own personal agendas and opinions about how the discernment should turn out, so the Spirit has the freedom to move within us.* Jesuits call this "holy indifference," which doesn't mean we don't care about the outcome. Rather, it means we are going into the discernment with an open mind and are agreeing to be surprised by how the Spirit moves in the group.

Holy indifference can be especially hard for clergy and lay church leaders, who may have a vision or a long-range plan for the congregation and want to persuade the others toward their preferred outcome. Because this is so hard, Ignatius advises us that if we find we are having trouble giving up our preferences, we are to pray for the *desire* for this indifference. We can offer a prayer much like that of the sick child's father to Jesus, "I believe. Help my unbelief!" (Mark 9:24). In our case, we would pray, "I want things my way. Help my lack of indifference!"

There are many other features to Ignatian discernment, and our Congregational Spiritual Road Map will include a process gleaned from Ignatius's writings, which have been used for centuries. It has been adapted from Ignatius's writing, using contemporary language, and many variations can be found in books on Christian spiritual discernment.

## THE SOCIAL DISCERNMENT CYCLE

Another Ignatian-adapted discernment process for congregations, communities, organizations, and institutions is the Social Discernment Cycle, described by Elizabeth Liebert. This process was created by spirituality professionals in the early 1990s to help institutions and organizations marry contemplation with social-justice action.

The Social Discernment Cycle (SDC) recognizes the congregation as a structure with a system—an intertwined group of relationships forming an entity that begins to have a life of its own, regardless of the individuals who move in and out of it.[3] As Liebert puts it, "The Social Discernment Cycle is designed to address large and small systems, to help us take concrete steps in the face of systemic complexity, be it in one's family, workplace, neighborhood, school, or church, in local or national politics, or in response to the global ecological crisis."[4]

Many times, organizations don't spend time understanding the many relationships, roles, power dynamics, beliefs, and patterns of behavior at work. The SDC helps congregations take a deep dive into who they are and who their neighbor is by asking profound, honest questions about topics like these:

- Roles and responsibilities individuals have in the congregation (both formal and informal), including who really has the power in the organization, how that power is exercised, and who is commonly left out

- Common patterns of behavior in the congregation

- The history of the congregation as well as its mission, vision, values, and traditions

- Social relationships within the congregation and how they function

- Scripture, theology, and ethical underpinnings of the congregation, both stated and unstated

- The ways this congregation feels invited to respond to all of the above, in either a transformative decision or a shift in understanding

A brief rundown of the phases of the process is included in the Congregational Spiritual Road Map at the end of this chapter.

## LEARNING FROM QUAKERS

About 141 years after Ignatius founded the Jesuit order, George Fox, a bright but unschooled British shoemaker, got fed up with institutional church, set out to find the plain truth of the gospel, and ended up founding the Religious Society of Friends, better known as Quakers. Fox roamed the countryside of England, preaching and teaching a simple faith based on paying attention to direct experiences of God in silence.

He writes of one mystical experience: "I heard a voice which said, 'There is one, even Christ Jesus, that can speak to thy condition;' and when I heard it my heart did leap for joy."[5] And with that, Fox traveled the countryside teaching and preaching that the light of Christ is in each of us, speaking to our condition and offering us joy. Fox reminds us to pay attention to our Inner Teacher.

The Quaker way of discernment is simple. For most Quaker individuals, discernment involves silent prayer and waiting for an answer, a sense of peace and clarity, or—to use their seventeenth-century words—watching for a "way to open." Patience and silence can be difficult for many of us, so the Quaker way of discernment, especially in community, takes practice. The clearness committee (covered in this chapter's Congregational Spiritual Road Map) is the most structured practice of Quaker discernment.

Quakers have written much about communities waiting for a leading from God. When discerning as a community, the group watches for a sense of unity around a way forward. Unity is not the same as complete agreement on the next step. When a group achieves unity, everyone agrees that the Spirit seems to be moving in a particular direction, and even if the next step is not every person's preferred action, no one feels compelled to stand in the way. In the same way, if someone feels such conviction that an action is not a true leading from God, he or she is obligated to speak against it. In that situation, Quakers continue discerning until unity is reached.

## MAKING YOUR OWN WAY

Whether your congregation or discernment work group uses an Ignatian process, clearness committee, or some hybrid, we urge you to stay with discernment until you experience unity. The essence of what you seek is the clarity and peace of knowing that what you are choosing *seems good to the Holy Spirit and to you.*

You may be saying to yourself, "That could take a while in my church." And you would typically be right. We aren't told how long the Council of Jerusalem lasted, but it is safe to assume that following any discernment process in community and waiting for a sense of unity around a path forward—especially on difficult questions—will take a mix of prayer, deep listening, ongoing dialogue and sometimes debate, silence, some changes of heart, inspiration, and patience. It will take love for one another and a willingness to relinquish agendas you may be holding onto, to stand aside and let a new path emerge.

## CONGREGATIONAL SPIRITUAL ROAD MAP FOR DISCERNMENT

Before beginning any discernment process, determine how many people will be involved. If you have a tiny church, you could involve the entire congregation. But we recommend that most congregations create a discernment task group of no more than eight to ten people who will commit to see the process through. And we recommend the process remain confidential until the group is ready to present their conclusion. This will lessen rumors and misinformation that can sometimes lead to conflict.

This task group could be asked to make the final decision, but it may instead make recommendations and share findings from the process to a governing body for final approval. For situations where the discernment group must report to someone, chapter 4 will describe how to effectively communicate your discernment conclusions to that person or group of decision makers.

Make sure the group carrying out your congregation's discernment process is as diverse as possible. The Council of Jerusalem included people with greatly divergent views on what was required to be a Christian. Include devoted longtime members and some of your "casually committed" in the discernment task group. Add the person who always plays devil's advocate. Bring in old and young people; people from all walks of life, ethnicities, and theological backgrounds; and longtime members and newcomers. Those designing the process always need to ask, "Who have we *not* invited to the table but should?" Marginalized people are frequently left out of church decision making, even though we know Jesus said, "The last shall be first."

## DISCERNMENT, IGNATIAN STYLE

One of the most important tools for discernment is a process assembled from writings found in Ignatius's *Spiritual Exercises*, a book for spiritual directors—in his day, priests—leading people through a lengthy guided retreat.[6] The retreat covers a lot more than discernment, but teachers of discernment use a section on "making an election" (Ignatius's term for making a faithful, informed decision) to create these processes. The process we describe here is an adaptation inspired by the teachings of Elizabeth Liebert.[7]

One person will facilitate the process. (Many organizations hire an outside facilitator to oversee and advise on matters of process.) Consider breaking the work up into several gatherings of at least two hours each. At the end of each session, check in with how individuals are feeling about the content and the process.[8]

## Begin with Prayer

Since this entire process is devoted to discovering God's desire for your group, encourage the group to spend time in personal prayer prior to each gathering. Each person should use the mode of prayer that best fits for them. Also, at the beginning of every gathering, take a significant amount of time for prayer (at least ten minutes), and consider stopping in the middle for a "prayer break" as well. You are seeking a collective sense of consolation in your discernment, so ask God for that gift.

## Clarify the Question

Discernment centers on a question, a choice, or a set of options. It should be concrete and understandable. Your group may spend a good deal of time honing the question. You might need to answer a number of questions before you can get to the core question. If that's the case, figure out what you need to know first before going deeper into your core question.

If your discernment group already has a firm grasp of the question, skip down to the next section. If you are not clear what the question is or which question comes first, complete the rest of this step. First, as individuals, consider the following questions: What is the challenge before us? Why have we gathered as a group for discernment?

Again as individuals, reflect on the following question: When you think from your deepest, truest self, what is your desire in this challenge? Keep your answer concrete and as specific as possible. Here are some examples of specific and concrete questions:

• Is God leading us to add a new facility to our grounds?

• Is it God's desire that we merge with another congregation?

• Is God asking us to refocus our mission? And if so, in what way are we invited to change?

• Is God asking us to let go of a particular program that is not thriving?

Next, individuals share their desires with the group. As a group, discuss these questions:

• What do you notice?

• What themes are taking shape?

• Does a concrete question for discernment emerge for your group from these desires?

Do your best to focus on what God is asking of the congregation, even if that is hard to determine.

### Prepare to Face the Question

Now is when that "holy indifference" Ignatian taught about comes into play. It is important that everyone let go of their preferred plans, agendas, and advice about the answer to the question under consideration.

Ask yourselves: Can we remain open to any outcome? If not, can everyone pray for God to help them with that? Does the group really want to know what God desires in this situation?

If fear or some other issue blocks the necessary "holy indifference," acknowledge that and pray for freedom so the Spirit can show the way forward.

## Attend to Practical Matters

Facts, details, and data are important. This is the time for homework assignments, with each person researching a different aspect of the question.[9] Explore the following issues in detail:

• What beliefs and values affect this question?

• What do we need to know to make this choice?

• What are the practical matters around this choice?

• What are the pros and cons for each choice we face? Evaluate each pro and con, and determine if some carry more weight than others.

• Who do we need to discuss this question with?

• What other parties may be affected by our decision?

• What individuals or groups of people might we be overlooking?

## Notice Intuition and Body Senses

As we practice discernment, we go beyond the facts. "We know far more than our conscious minds process; intuition collects data that is outside of our conscious awareness and presents it to our conscious mind for its consideration," writes Liebert.[10] She suggests that silence, openness to images, and gut feelings give us information for discernment. If that doesn't work, she says, try an artistic outlet such as drawing, writing, or even dancing.

This step invites us to allow the wisdom in our body speak to the question. This will be easier for some people than others, but everyone can pay attention to how the question "sits with them" physically. Take this session in three parts:

1. Ask discerners to listen in silent prayer (allow at least twenty minutes) to their intuition around the options your group faces. Some people may need to walk around, stretch, or go outside for this step.

2. Again, in silence, invite them to listen to their body's "felt senses." These could include pain, tension, twinges, agitation, or relaxation. People may find images emerge, such as "When I consider this option, I feel like I have a rock in my gut."

3. Ask the group to share what happened for them in those two times of prayer. Allow a few moments of silence between each respondent. What does the group notice? Is there a common theme or a sense of direction coming from intuition and felt senses?

### Imagine Outcomes

One of the hallmarks of Ignatian spirituality is its use of the imagination. Ignatius wanted people to put themselves in Bible stories and imagine what it would be like to be in that place and to converse with characters in the story. He also suggested we use our imaginations in discernment. He offered three scenarios that can be used for guided meditation.[11] (Allow at least ten minutes for the imagination prayer in each scenario and even longer for sharing.)

1. **The advice-giving test.** Imagine that someone you respect from another congregation asks you for advice about the

same situation. What would you feel most comfortable advising them to do?

2. **The rocking-chair test.** Imagine it is many years in the future. The leadership of your congregation is reflecting on the decision you made on the question before you now and has invited you to talk about how that discernment was done. How do you describe the options you had? Which option would you feel most able to explain and defend? Which option has the most integrity for you?

3. **The judgment day test.** Imagine you are facing God or Christ on the last day and you are asked how your congregation answered this discernment question. Which option would you feel proud to have chosen?

### Make the Choice

Once you have done all of the preceding activities, checked in with one another about how you are feeling about the discernment, and prayed together, it's time to make a choice. This is where the use of the Daily Examen over time comes in handy because it helps you identify consolation and desolation. You are looking for the choice that offers the most consolation. You are searching for which way *the group as one body* feels God is leading. What choice feels like the one God desires?

You certainly may try on the choice before making a final determination. Test it out by using your imagination. Set aside a period of time (it could be as long as a week) for individuals to imagine saying yes to each of your options. Imagine all the ramifications of that choice. You're not trying to predict the future. You're discovering more fully how you are sensing the answer in the present. For example, if a congregation is considering merging with another, the discernment group might take one week to sit with and pray about the congregations remaining as they are and then another week imagining them merged. Discerners are looking for which option seems to draw them closer to God, which one feels more like a fit, or which one appears more life-giving to them. For each option ask:

- In what ways do I feel consolation around this choice?

- In what ways do I feel desolation around this choice?

The final part of the Ignatian process takes place after you have made your decision (in the discerning body): taking action and evaluating the outcome. We take that up in detail in the next chapter.

## SOCIAL DISCERNMENT CYCLE

The social discernment cycle is a thorough, detailed discernment process and requires some preparation to lead. We recommend Elizabeth Liebert's *The Soul of Discernment* as the definitive guide to the theology, pedagogy, and practical use of the cycle. To offer you a brief look at this process, we obtained permission to reprint Liebert's condensed form of the Social Discernment Cycle.[12]

### Phase 1: Focus for Discernment

Pray for spiritual freedom.

Prayerfully select the system or clarify the aspect of the system that will be the focus of the discernment.

### Phase 2: Current Situation

Pray for spiritual freedom.

Describe the concrete instances of the roles, behaviors, environment, and events in this structure, paying particular attention to the situation of the marginalized.

Note how you are responding physically, intellectually, emotionally, and spiritually.

### Phase 3: Social Analysis

Pray for spiritual freedom.

Identify the history, mission, traditions, and cultures of this system.

Describe the assumptions made by people in this structure, their social relationships, and the flow of power.

Note how you are feeling at this point.

### Phase 4: Prayer and Theological Reflection

Pray for spiritual freedom.

Spend some time in quiet prayer, just being present to God and to your structure; notice any new freedom in you.

What Scriptures connect to your sense of freedom?

What theological truths express this freedom?

Name what is graced and sinful in this structure and the transformation in you so far.

Note how you are feeling at this point.

### Phase 5: The Decision and Inner Confirmation

Reexperience the freedom from phase 4. If you do not experience freedom, repeat phase 4. What desires flow from your freedom?

Surface possible concrete responses you could make, and touch them against your spiritual freedom. Discard those that do not continue or strengthen your spiritual freedom.

Choose a response that you will implement first, and again touch it against your spiritual freedom.

Name the people who will be involved in carrying out the action.

What means will be used to evaluate it? When?

Carry out the action, noting the changes, both within you and within the structure, that happen as a result.

### Phase 6: Review and Structural Confirmation

Return to your experience of spiritual freedom.

Look back over the entire discernment process for places where you experienced significant resistance, discouragement, or disinclination to proceed. How did these shift?

Conversely, look for places where you experienced clarity,

consolation, energy to proceed. What can you learn from these shifts?

Look for indicators that the structure is moving Godward, such as greater justice, security, meaningful work, sustainable progress, cultural roots, unity, meaningful relationships, diversity, flexibility and so on.

Notice how your action has affected the marginalized, how power functions, and some possible results. Do these indicators suggest continuing?

If yes, conclude your discernment. If no, adjust your action accordingly or return to earlier phases of the discernment process.

Express gratitude for all that has transpired.

## DISCERNMENT, QUAKER STYLE

For Quakers, discernment is a central practice. Their monthly worship meeting for business is dedicated to listening to the Spirit for wisdom around their business questions. The Ohio Valley Yearly Meeting says this about discernment: "The Society of Friends believes that our best decisions are dependent on spiritual discernment. Therefore, it transacts its business by seeking unity under divine guidance rather than by majority vote or even consensus. This means in our business meetings, each contribution to the discussion is heard in a spirit of prayer. We listen lovingly and respectfully for the voice of God through what each person says."[13]

Two helpful concepts in Quaker discernment are "threshing sessions" and "clearness committee."

## Threshing Sessions

The agricultural term *threshing* refers to the low-tech winnowing process wheat farmers use to separate the usable wheat grain from the husks, called chaff. Farmers repeatedly toss the whole grain into the air, allowing the wheat to fall to the ground while the wind blows the chaff away. In the same way, Quakers hope that "grains of truth" will rest with them after a threshing session.

As a discernment technique, a threshing session is a meeting held prior to any difficult or complex discernment question, giving everyone a chance to speak their mind, if they desire, on issues surrounding the question. Threshing sessions help everyone get their agendas and hesitations out in the open. You need a facilitator, which Quakers call a clerk, to run the session. Knowledgeable people should attend to share factual information, answer questions, or explain complicated issues, and a recorder should take notes for later use, if necessary. No decisions are made at a threshing session. It's brainstorming at its best! And participants are to refrain from arguing or critiquing someone else's opinions at this gathering.

Here's a possible template for a threshing session in a congregation:

• The clerk opens with prayer and some silence, inviting those attending to spend a few moments reflecting on the question "What is it like for me to feel the presence of God?"

• The clerk explains what a threshing session is—a way to prepare the congregation for spiritual discernment around a critical question. It's a time to toss out your ideas, thoughts, and questions and see what grains of truth fall to the ground.

• The discernment question is presented. It should be as concrete and manageable as possible. Examples: Should we continue our after-school programming? Shall we sell our building? Do we add another person to our pastoral staff?

• The floor is opened for "threshing." Participants should use "I" statements and speak only for themselves, not referring to what someone else has said. Persons with particular knowledge about the facts surrounding the question may offer more information to help illuminate the question. The recorder will take notes or may use an audio-recording device to help prepare the report of what happened.

• The clerk makes sure everyone has an opportunity to speak. It is helpful to use the guideline that everyone must have a chance to speak once before anyone speaks a second time.

• At the end, the clerk reminds the group that no decisions are made at this meeting. The recorder may post the notes for all to read at a later time.

## The Clearness Committee

The Quaker clearness committee, based in silent prayer, is a gathering of people for a structured time of listening and discerning. In our highly verbal culture, the clearness committee takes some getting used to. It is a time when discerners break silence only in order to share how the Spirit moves them. Parker Palmer describes the practice of a clearness committee for individual discernment: "Each of us has an inner, divine light that gives us the guidance we need but is often obscured by sundry forms of inner and outer interference. The function of the clearness committee is not to give advice or alter and "fix" people but to help people remove obstacles and discover the divine assistance that is within."[14]

For our purposes, using the process for *communal* decisions, the function of the clearness committee is to overcome any obstacles and discover divine assistance within the group as a whole.

A clearness committee has important guidelines, and when everyone involved knows and accepts their role, follows the guidelines, and agrees to approach this as a prayerful time of exploration, it can be revelatory.

Each clearness committee session includes a time near the end of the process for assessing whether spiritual unity has been achieved. Traditionally in Quaker settings, the clerk names what they call "the sense of the meeting" and suggests if and when they believe unity is present. The group may confirm the clerk's sense, or it may disagree.

Unity requires that the group have a "sense" of the direction in which the Holy Spirit is leading. If it does not, another meeting may be held after some time for more prayer. A lack of unity may mean that some discerners in the clearness committee are holding to agendas they want to promote rather than submitting to the leading of the Holy Spirit. Again, prayer and openness to God's preferred outcome is called for. Unity is never about bullying or waiting for everyone to relent and be agreeable. It's about doing the best you can to determine in which direction the Spirit seems to be moving.

## Preparing for a Clearness Committee

Hold needed threshing sessions prior to planning the clearness committee. Decide what the discernment question for the committee will be, and assign someone knowledgeable about the issue to prepare background information naming the question and sharing pertinent facts about the question. Include a list of the guidelines in the statement, and send it to everyone involved in the clearness committee a few days prior. Ask them to pray with the question individually before attending.

Decide when, where, and how long the clearness committee will meet. Usually you need two to three hours (with a silent break after the first hour) in a quiet room that is large enough to hold a circle of chairs for participants. This process is not done at a conference room table. Think if it as a prayer gathering.

There are three important roles in clearness committee. Long before the planned gathering, decide who will be in those roles.

1. **Clerk.** One of the discerners serves as the clerk, who keeps time, monitors the pace, and makes sure the guidelines are being followed. An outside facilitator with experience in clearness committees may be hired to assume this role, which is advisable for groups not familiar with the clearness committee process.[15] The outside facilitator would not be a discerner but would share a sense of the meeting with the committee toward the end of the process.

2. **Discerners.** The people chosen to participate in the process are the discerners. Choose individuals who agree to pray about the question, hold "holy indifference" to the outcome, and are willing to follow the guidelines. They need to understand that they are primarily on hand to listen to the situation and question at hand, pray, keep silence, and when appropriate, share leadings they believe come from divine assistance within.

3. **Recorder.** One person serves as the recorder, who writes up what is said in committee. An audio-recording device may be used. This information is solely for use by the committee and not to be shared outside of

the committee, unless everyone agrees to allow that. The recorder may also be a discerner.

Note that, prior to meeting, it helps if everyone involved has read some information about the clearness committee. Since there are many ways to adapt the clearness committee process, reading about it can help congregational leaders adapt the method and guidelines that work best for your group. The following are short, helpful writings about clearness committees;

- The Center for Courage and Renewal has a web page on the clearness committee that includes an article by Parker Palmer, "The Clearness Committee: A Communal Approach to Discernment in Retreats."[16] This article is a classic description of the clearness committee and includes an adaptation for use in retreats.

- "Clearness Committees and Their Use in Personal Discernment" is a paper about individuals' use of the clearness committee,[17] but it has a lot of good information to help a group get ready for the process.

- "Spiritual Discernment: The Context and Goal of Clearness Committees," by Patricia Loring, is a Pendle Hill pamphlet available at www.pendlehill.org.[18]

### Guidelines for a Clearness Committee

For an effective clearness committee everyone must agree to a set of important guidelines. The following are the most common examples of the guidelines used by facilitators of clearness committees.

1. The clerk is the guardian of the guidelines and gently intercedes when they are not followed.

2. Discerners are to share only insights, leadings, or other

reflections about the discernment question that arise during the time of silent prayer. Discerners are not to comment directly on anything already shared. They are not to respond to, refer to, restate, or refute what someone has shared.

3.  Discerners will not in any way try to "fix" a situation, give advice, or "set anyone straight" about anything. A clearness committee is not a brainstorming session; a threshing session would be the time for that work.

4.  Discerners take care that what they share is prompted by their prayer insights or the urging of the Spirit and not simply their ego.

5.  Discerners are mindful of the need for silence between persons sharing. The clerk may ask for periods of silence if the committee moves too fast.

6.  Discerners do not share their insight if another has already shared it. Instead, they rest in the joy that the Spirit has spoken the same word to more than one person.

7.  To allow everyone an opportunity to be heard, every discerner is given a chance to share once before anyone is permitted to share a second time.

8.  After a period of time in the clearness committee (the length decided ahead of time), the clerk has the option to offer their sense of the meeting, sharing whether and to what degree they sense unity has been reached. The clerk then asks the committee to reflect on whether unity or clarity around the discernment question has been reached. If there is a sense of unity, the recorder will note that, using wording for the sense that the group agrees upon. If there is no sense of

unity (a common occurrence), it is not failure. It simply means more discernment and prayer are needed.

9.  The committee agrees to confidentiality around what has been shared. Once unity is reached, the committee agrees on what to share with a wider audience.

### Suggested Process for Clearness Committee Clerk

As people gather, greet them and ask them to take a seat in the circle.

Call the meeting to order, and go over a brief outline of the process. Read over the guidelines in the preceding list, and make sure all discerners agree to them. Let discerners know you will be the keeper of the time, pace, and guidelines and that you will gently redirect or correct them if the guidelines are being overlooked.

Begin with a brief spoken prayer and ten minutes of silence before introducing the question and its background.

State the question and its background. If you, the clerk, are not the person who prepared the statement of the question and background, you may ask the person who did so to share it with the group. Allow the committee about ten minutes to ask any simple clarifying questions they may have about the background or question. (This is not the time for opinion or substantive sharing, only points of clarification.)

Take another period of silent prayer (about five to ten minutes) for the committee to sit with the question and background. Let them know that you will ring a chime at the end of the silence.

When the silence ends, remind the committee of the importance of maintaining a contemplative pace—long periods of silence between sharing. Participants are to share only what they sense God is inviting them to share around the question. Open the floor for discerners to share these prayer insights, images, desires, blocks, or questions. The recorder will make note of all statements or questions. If a question arises that can easily be answered by a person on the committee, it may be answered (at the clerk's request). However, the clerk should take care to maintain the contemplative and open atmosphere, and the person answering should answer only the question with the facts at hand, not give an opinion.

Allow about an hour for responses. If things begin to move fast, with little or no silence between responses, the clerk should call for a return to silence. The floor will close until the clerk reopens it. These silent pauses help discerners relax and return to listening to God.

After this long period of responding, take a ten- to fifteen-minute silent break, allowing people to stretch, walk around, get snacks, and visit the restrooms.

Reconvene the committee with silence (three to four minutes). If you need to remind the group of any guidelines, do so now.

About twenty minutes prior to ending time, take a time of silence (five minutes) for everyone to reflect on whether they sense unity in the group around the question. At the end of the silence, you, the clerk, may offer your sense of the meeting. Then, open the floor for others to confirm your sense or share why they do not sense unity. (Remember, unity does not mean everyone agrees completely on every detail. It means everyone agrees the Spirit is moving in a particular direction and they are not inclined to stand in the way.) Unity may be present around some aspects of the question but not others. Have the recorder write down whatever the committee agrees is the sense of the meeting. If clarity and unity have been reached, then that is what is reported. If there is no sense of unity, more discernment and perhaps another clearness committee are called for in the future. If so, set the date and time for the next gathering.

The clerk ends the meeting with more silence or asks everyone in the circle to share one word that expresses their experience of the clearness committee gathering.

After the meeting, the recorder sends committee members a write-up of what was shared in the circle and what they agreed the sense of the meeting to be. The recorder also confirms any further committee gatherings scheduled.

## DISCERNMENT, YOUR WAY

You may find after reading about Jesuit and Quaker spirituality that you are inspired to come up with your own process. It may take a little more work to develop a process, but you'll certainly be invested in it, and if it goes well, it could become a tradition in your community. Consider combining exercises and practices that may already be familiar to the congregation with a few that are unfamiliar. Respecting the familiar will create the trust you need before asking the congregation to stretch and try something new.

When creating your own discernment process, make sure you are covering the following twelve principles, gleaned from both Ignatian and Quaker spirituality. Each has a corresponding question or two to consider:

1. Discernment hinges on a concrete question, a choice between two or more options. *What is the question we need to discern?*

2. Spiritual discernment is steeped in prayer, which includes waiting in silence. *How are we praying about this question? What emerges as a result of our prayer?*

3. Good discernment listens to the congregation's truest and deepest desires. *What do we most want in our life together? How do these options satisfy those deep desires?*

4. To discern well, we need to listen carefully to the "movements of the heart" in daily life. *What events, moments, or decisions give our community deep peace, gratitude, energy, love, and joy (consolation)? What events, moments, or decisions give our community anxiety, chaos, despair, and deadness (desolation)?*

5. Good discernment leaves the outcome open and in God's hands. *Can we be at peace with whatever God shows us in this discernment, regardless of outcome? Can we humbly lay down our preferences in favor of what is revealed to us in the discernment? If not, do we at least desire to be open to God's revelation in this matter? (If the answer to that question is no, then we pray for the desire to be open.)*

6. We need to be relatively free spiritually (from fear, addiction, compulsion) in order to discern well. *What fears, destructive habits, or blocks are getting in the way of exploring this question?*

7. To discern well, church leaders need a thorough knowledge of the options and practical considerations. *What are the facts surrounding the question? Whose lives*

are affected by these options? What are the pros and cons for each option? Do some of these pros and cons have greater weight than others?

8. The options under consideration must be weighed using head, heart, and body wisdom. *Which option feels most rational to us? Which one speaks to the heart of the congregation? Which option "just feels right"? As we consider this choice, what are we experiencing in our bodies? (Notice if most or all experience a similar bodily sensation.)*

9. Discernment involves imagining making a choice and reflecting on the future. *If we make this choice now, how might we feel, act, or be in the future? How does thinking about this choice make us feel right now?*

10. Christian spiritual discernment always considers how the option under consideration affects the faith community, its partners, the surrounding community, and people who are poor, forgotten, and hurting. *How is our choice advancing God's reign in the world? How is our choice affecting people who have fewer choices than we do? Who benefits? Who is left out?*

11. Discernment doesn't go on forever. At some point, you must take action. You may make a preliminary choice and sit with it before taking action. *As we make the choice, do we feel a sense of lasting peace? Where do we feel alive and open to the Spirit? Where do we feel dull or blocked?*

12. Good discernment is evaluated later, as the "fruit of the Spirit" (or not!) emerges. *What has been the outcome of making this choice? Do we still feel consolation around the choice? Do we need to do more discernment?*

If you use these principles as a guide, your process will be balanced and comprehensive.

## EVALUATING PROGRESS

The best outcome for any discernment process is a decision that has the support of all who were involved in making it. Here are some ways to reflect on your decision:

- Did the discernment process draw us closer to God?

- Did the process draw us closer to one another?

- What did we learn along the way?

- When did we feel a deep connection with the holy?

- When did we feel desolation or brokenness?

- How is the fruit of the Spirit evident in the decision? (For examples of this "fruit," see Gal 5:22, which lists love, joy, peace, gentleness, goodness, faith, meekness, temperance.)

Once your congregation has come to a decision, it's time to move into action. That's the topic of our next chapter and the next stop on our Congregational Spiritual Road Trip.

# 4

## Action

I appointed you to go and bear fruit, fruit that will last.
—John 15:16b

Discernment is the what and why of congregational spirituality. Action is the fruit of this work. It is the concrete plan—the who, how, and when—of living out what you discover when you discern.

One of the complaints about any contemplative approach is that it takes too much time. Yes, the contemplative approach can be lengthy. But how long does it take to untangle from a bad decision made in haste? In the long run, taking the contemplative approach will often save you time.

Another complaint comes from people who have seen discernment processes accomplish little or nothing. But, if our discernment work never moves us to action, then we're not doing it right!

If you have worked your way through the Congregational Spiritual Road Map this far and have come to clarity on a discernment question, congratulations! You've achieved a lot and hopefully discovered one part of your church's calling. This chapter is about some of the issues you face once you have heard that call.

## WE DISCERNED—NOW WHAT?

Before beginning any action on your goal, take time to step back from your work to observe and reflect again on where you feel consolation or desolation. Ask:

- What fruit of the Spirit have we experienced in our time spent imagining the options?

- Do we experience spiritual freedom in our choice? How were individuals able to set aside their preferences or blocks in order to feel free?

- Do we feel confident we have reached a sense of unity in the matter? How have we determined this sense of unity? What are its markers?

- Does part of the discernment need revisiting? Do we need to retrace any steps? What areas need to be stronger?

It's not a sign of failure if you need to revise. Discernment is art and mystery, not science! You can always go back and work on sections that seem incomplete.

Once you are ready to move from discernment to action, take time to celebrate the work of coming to a faithful, considered choice. Offer prayers of gratitude for all you have received from God while moving through this discernment. And ask for guidance through the next important phase: activation.

## WHAT IS THE ACTION?

Once clear on the action to be taken, the discernment group or a designated scribe writes up a report including the conclusion and any background information pertinent to the decision to be presented to anyone in charge of final approval. From this review and writing, you should be able to give a short, clear answer to the question *What did you all come up with in your discernment?* (your "elevator speech").

The elevator speech will be the core of what you present to others. Once it is written, make copies for everyone involved in the discernment process. The Congregational Spiritual Road Map at the end of this chapter will give you a template and examples to help in writing this conclusion.

Unless your entire congregation was in on the discernment process, the group tasked with doing the discernment will need to make a presentation to the larger congregation. This could be a written report, an oral report by one or more people from the discernment group, a visual presentation, or all of these. In our experience, the more information you freely share with the larger body, the more trust they have in the work you did.[1] Here's what you will want to share with the congregation:

- How you prayed throughout the process, perhaps including an experience or two from prayer

- A brief description of the process you chose to use, including the various stages

- Places where your discernment group felt spiritual consolation and desolation (familiar concepts, because you introduced the congregation to the prayer of examen in the reflection phase of the journey), including how those spiritual movements helped you come to the conclusion you reached

- The conclusion and how you reached unity on the conclusion

The road map for this chapter will offer suggestions for presenting discernment agreements to a congregation. Even if the discernment group was given the task of making the final decision (as opposed to offering a recommendation), allow your congregation time to sit with and pray with the results. You'll want to be sure that the congregation embraces the discernment conclusion and understands the sense of unity you achieved.

More than likely, your discernment group presents the conclusion as a recommendation to the church's governing body or congregation as a whole. Consider everyone involved in the discernment process an ambassador for the process. Ask them to be ready to share highlights of the process with church members and leadership. If your discernment group embodies the unity found in the process, people in the congregation will be encouraged and perhaps intrigued. They might even want to be in the next discernment task group after seeing how energized you are from finding unity through a contemplative spiritual practice.

## WHAT IF THE FINAL DECISION IS NOT UP TO THE CONGREGATION?

Your congregation may make a decision on an important matter but be required to have it reviewed or approved by a bishop or judicatory body. If your congregation doesn't have the final word on changes you want to make, the outcome of your discernment will have to go through another layer of discernment.

The process for presenting your findings to a governing body is the same as that for presenting to your congregation. If possible, have everyone on the discernment task group meet in person with the judicatory person or group that will have the final say. If that's not possible, then send your group leader and perhaps one more articulate ambassador.

It is possible that when you present all the work you have done and talk about the deep spiritual connections you all made to come to the conclusion, the ruling person or body will hear in your presentation the voice of the Spirit and agree with your findings. However, if it doesn't work out that way, don't despair. This outcome could point to one of the following needs:

- More discernment is needed on *their* part. Give them as much information as possible, and allow them time to pray and discern. Find out if they need more information about any particular part of the decision. Be helpful and hopeful.

- More discernment is needed on *your* part. Make note of any places where the ruling person or body is not in agreement with your discernment. Take those issues back into discernment. Perhaps they have some wisdom you did not have access to during your process.

- A compromise may need to be found. Ask if they are willing to discern with you to find a sense of unity in this new situation.

## ADDRESSING CONFLICT

Conflict happens. It isn't bad or sinful. It means people care deeply about a situation. The Congregational Spiritual Road Map includes a section on conflict resolution, which can help you navigate difficulties in the discernment or action phase of your journey.

## OVERVIEW OF MOVING INTO ACTION

After receiving any clearance needed for your discernment, you can begin organizing for action. You are moving from the big idea to smaller, measurable tasks that will be assigned to people for completion by a due date. You may use any template or process your congregation has for mapping action, especially if you find it helpful and effective. If you haven't been using detailed written action plans, now is the time to start.

Your discernment has now become an action project, and to complete it, you will name several goals, listed in the order to be completed. Each goal will include tasks to be completed, and those will be placed on a goal assignment worksheet. Your final work as a discernment group will include the following steps:

- Create a project work group, which is different from the discernment group but ideally includes some people from the discernment group, at least as advisers.

- Create a prioritized list of goals for the project. Once you have done this, you may opt to turn the next task over to the project work group.

- Create a detailed goal assignment worksheet containing a description of tasks to be done, names of those who have agreed to do each task, and due dates.

- Evaluate the progress of the project.

Once you have formed the project work group, appoint a small team within it to keep track of the assignments. As mentioned before, you may use the resources included in the Congregational Spiritual Road Map for implementing your decision, or you may come up with your own. Perhaps someone in your church has experience in using a planning tool and can guide you in setting up a realistic plan of action.

## WHO IS DOING THE TASKS?

The project work group estimates how many people they will need to complete each task in a timely manner. It will take time to discover who feels called to do each task on the worksheet. Please don't do what so many churches do: decide to take on an enormous project, begin with a few true believers and a lot of wishful thinking, and then panic when the original crew burns out and many more volunteers are needed to get the work done. One true test of a calling is the presence of energy to carry it out.[2]

Never coerce volunteers. If you have to beg people to volunteer, it may be a sign that more discernment is needed. Be patient and prayerful. It will take time to find people who have the gifts and skills for the tasks and for them to know if they feel called to do the work. A detailed rundown of a suggested calling process is found in this chapter's road map.

## HOW WILL WE KNOW THE WORK HAS BEEN COMPLETED?

On your goal assignment worksheet, give a brief description of the specific markers for the completion of each task. It can be difficult for those who take assignments to know precisely what they have agreed upon. The descriptions need to be specific and clear about what they are to do and what constitutes completion of a task.

## WHEN SHOULD WE BE FINISHED?

The project work group needs a timeline for measurable action with due dates for each task to be completed. If someone cannot complete their task by the due date, they may need help or an extension on their due date.

From this point on, it's just a matter of doing the work. It's gratifying to see what was a desire and sense of call in the discernment phase become a reality in action. Once your work is done, use the evaluation tool at the end of the Congregational Spiritual Road Map.

## CONGREGATIONAL SPIRITUAL ROAD MAP FOR ACTION

Now that we've gone over the basic process for moving into action, here is the Congregational Spiritual Road Map with more details.

### WRITE YOUR ELEVATOR SPEECH

Craft a *brief* statement about the discernment that is suitable for publication in the congregational newsletter. You don't need a lot of detail—just the decision. Here are a few examples:

#### Project: Two Churches Merging

A discernment group made up of people from both Glory Methodist and Grace Lutheran spent four months considering God's desire for the future of these two churches. We feel a strong sense of unity and consolation around recommending that the two congregations merge. We recommend an action plan for this merger be developed with a target date of January 5 for a celebration of the completed merger.

#### Project: Church Closing

The discernment task group for Covenant United Church of Christ finished our work with a sad but clear sense that Covenant's life as we have known it has come to its end and that God is leading us to legally dissolve our status as a church and bequeath our worldly assets to future new church starts in this region.

## Project: Becoming Open and Affirming of LGBTQ Persons

The seven members of New Life Presbyterian Church's discernment group recommend this congregation become a member of the More Light Network of Presbyterians and work toward the full participation of LGBTQIA+ people in the life, ministry, and witness of the Presbyterian Church (USA) and in society. As we prayed and gathered information about the full inclusion of LGBTQIA+ persons, we felt an undeniable sense of unity and a clear sense of God's desire for this church to make a strong open-and-affirming statement.

### CREATE YOUR ACTION PLAN

Next, you will move from vision to planning. To illustrate how a congregation might take action after discernment, let's look at a hypothetical case and consider each step along the way. A discernment group from Church of New Hope spent several months considering whether they were being called to "nest" a congregation—that is, offer their space, expertise, and financial support to the pastor and leadership of one of their denomination's struggling new church starts. Their prayer and work in discernment led to a unified yes on this question.

### Step One: Naming the Action

The polity of Church of New Hope is independent congregational, so its decision needed no approval from the denomination. The discernment group was charged with presenting to the congregation its outcome and how it arrived at yes. They developed the following elevator speech:

> After much prayer and information gathering, the discernment task group of Church of New Hope believes our congregation has

the resources, energy, and calling from God to nurture and support this new church in our denomination.

## Step Two: Getting the Necessary Approval

The discerners used presentation software to create a slide show for the congregation to consider before final approval. The slide show explained the many phases of the discernment process and included stories of how the discerners' times of prayer increased their sense of consolation around offering the church's building and support to this new start. They shared the logistics: the new church already has a pastor, receives some financial support from the denomination, and hopes to spend no more than one year nested at Church of New Hope before acquiring or renting a new space. The discernment group also shared an estimate of how much financial aid the new start would probably need from Church of New Hope, what the specific needs of the new church were expected to be, and approximately how many volunteers would be needed to make the nesting possible.

At the congregational meeting, church members had an opportunity to ask questions, and those on the task group were able to share information they obtained during their research phase. The discerners then shared the recommendation, and the congregation voted to move forward with the plan to nest the new church.

After the vote, the presentation concluded with a brief outline of the action plan.

## Step Three: Creating the List of Goals

After the vote, the Church of New Hope decided to create a project work group that included a few members of the discernment task force to determine what needed to be done to achieve the goal of nesting a new congregation. They created an assignment worksheet for each of the four goals:

1. Welcome the new-start pastor (see sample worksheet).

2. Prepare our physical space for use by a new community.

3. Seek volunteers for assisting the project work group on its tasks.

4. Raise funds to assist the new start as it grows.

A blank version of this worksheet appears at the end of this chapter for your own use.

### Church of New Hope Goal Assignment Worksheet

| Goal: Welcome pastor of the new church start | | | |
|---|---|---|---|
| **Task** | **Who will do it** | **How we will know it's done** | **When it should be completed** |
| Arrange to meet the pastor for coffee | Mel | Meeting will be scheduled and everyone contacted | March 10 |
| Interview representatives from three churches who have nested new starts to find out what their experience was like | Sue | She will report back to the project work group at the next meeting | March 20 |
| Obtain denominational resources re: new church starts | Thelma | She will give a report at the next meeting | March 10 |

## Step Four: Prepare Task Descriptions
## and Recruit Volunteers

The project work group of Church of New Hope prayed together and made a list of people with particular gifts for each goal: welcoming the new-start pastor; cleaning, beautifying, and preparing the physical space for newcomers; recruiting volunteers; and fund-raising. The work group divided up the list of names and made personal invitations to those on the list, asking them to pray about the possibility of serving on the project work group.

## Step Five: Define Tasks

The project work group then created an assignment worksheet for each goal, outlining the tasks to be completed. For each task, they indicated "how we know when the work is completed." For example, the task list for fund-raising includes this task:

> Susan has agreed to coordinate fund-raising for the new church start. She will have completed the task when she has made one presentation to the congregation asking for donations and has approached twenty individuals asking for contributions.

## Step Six: Set Completion Dates

For each task on the goal assignment worksheet, the project work group specifies a completion date. In the previous example of fund-raising, the worksheet indicates that Susan will have completed her assignment by March 25.

## IMPLEMENT YOUR ACTION PLAN

When the planning is complete, the work gets under way,

with a subset of the project work group assigned to oversee the progress.

The action growing out of discernment is complete when Church of New Hope celebrates the grand opening of worship for the new church start.

## INVITE PEOPLE TO SERVE

Here is a template for finding the right people for the implementation of your action plan. It is adapted from Mark Yaconelli's book *Contemplative Youth Ministry:*[3]

1. Create a description for the volunteer position you will be filling.

2. Pray for the Spirit to assist you in inviting the most gifted people for this task.

3. Brainstorm and list several names of people for each task. Ask the pastor to help with this list.

4. Choose who you will call first and make personal invitations to each of your top choices, giving them a clear description of the work to be done and asking them to take time (about two weeks) to pray about the possibility and to say yes only if they feel called to take on and complete the task. It's important that no one feel coerced into doing a job that someone else determined was necessary.

5. If you do not find people for each of the jobs, repeat steps 1 to 3. Don't begin the project or task until you have the right people on board.

6. Consider bringing all the workers together for regular prayer and discernment on smaller issues that crop up along the way.

7. Build accountability by getting informal reports on how the work is coming along.

## CONTEMPLATIVE PRACTICES
## AND CONFLICT TRANSFORMATION

Conflict, usually based in anxiety or fear, has the potential to derail a discernment or work group process. But it doesn't have to. For those leading the group, it's important to model ways to approach conflict in a welcoming, peaceful way. It may sound counterintuitive to welcome conflict, but the more we see these bumps in the road as a normal part of the journey—just another challenge—the more we are able to help people navigate through their fears.

Pastoral counselor and church consultant Ronald Richardson says, "The job of effective church leaders is to help keep down the level of anxiety in the emotional system of the congregation. When things are calmer, people are able to think more clearly about their options in the midst of stressful circumstances and develop a reasonable, workable plan of action."[4] Richardson says the leader can reduce organizational stress by modeling how a non-anxious presence responds. Contemplative practices can help everyone calm down and support a process for moving through conflict so you can get on with your discernment.

When groups work through conflict in a healthy way, they grow stronger. So when it appears, face it head-on with compassion and courage, understanding that change commonly brings on conflict in congregations.

Spiritual work such as discernment can unearth unresolved conflict or lead to a new one. If your group experiences conflict, don't terminate your work in frustration. Instead, pause it, and work on the conflict before resuming.

There are many ways to approach conflict resolution. The discernment processes outlined in chapter 3 can be used with the question centering around the conflict and how it can be resolved. Or your congregation may already have some conflict resolution practices that you know and trust.

The following contemplative practices and suggestions can help everyone calm down and support a process for moving through conflict so you can get on with your discernment. At the first sign of unrest, go back to chapter 1, "Awareness of God," and lead the group through some contemplative exercises that help lower stress and draw their attention away from their preferences or complaints and onto God. Additionally, try the following exercises.

### Exploring Fear

Roger Walsh's book *Essential Spirituality* includes a practice that invites us to stop avoiding fear and instead befriend it. This, he says, can take away its power and lead to healing.[5]

Begin by taking a moment to relax and get comfortable where you are seated. Take several deep, slow breaths.

Now let yourself feel the fear and explore it. Where do you feel it in your body? Is there an image to describe your fear? Or a word? Does your fear bring back a memory? Don't worry if nothing happens in this step. Just let yourself feel the fear.

If an image or word does emerge, explore it. Be curious. Notice your posture and where you might be holding tension. Slow your breathing, and see if you can allow your tense muscles to relax even as you consider your experience of fear.

After some more deep breaths, check in with the fear. What does it feel like? Look like? Has it changed?

Continue to relax. Releasing tension helps release the fear.

The release of fear is your mind healing. Continue to breathe slowly and release tension in your body. Notice how the fear dissolves.

End with a prayer of gratitude to God for the self-healing work that comes with awareness and relaxation.

## Reflecting on Two Questions

A helpful way of lowering anxiety around conflict is to apply principles of nonviolent communication identified by Marshall Rosenberg.[6] He has an interesting exercise called "the two questions," which helps people turn attention to what is important. In times of conflict, have members reflect quietly on these questions:[7]

- What's alive in us?
- What can we do to make life more wonderful?

## Compassionate Breathing

The compassionate-breathing exercise comes from *A Practical Guide to Mindfulness-Based Compassionate Living*, by Erik van den Brink and Frits Koster.[8] It can be used when a group is feeling hurt or is suffering as a result of conflict.

Let yourself be present to any hurt or suffering with open, kind awareness.

Allow your breath to find a soothing rhythm.

Breathe in what hurts; breathe out what heals. Allow your out-breath to transform whatever suffering you have taken on.

## Conflict Transformation Process

The following process is for conflicts that are at the problem-solving stage, meaning the people involved are open about the problem, are able to stay focused on it, and have the objective of coming to an agreement. Once a conflict gets to the point where people are refusing to hear one another or seeking to win an argument, you will need a trained mediation expert.

Regardless of the level of conflict at hand, you will need one person in the role of mediator to facilitate the process. These steps are adapted from the Lombard Mennonite Peace Center training manual for the Mediation Skills Training Institute.[9]

**Step 1: Introduction.** The mediator explains the steps to be taken and their role as mediator. For example: "I'd like to tell you what happens during mediation. Everyone will have a chance to talk about the situation as you see it. We'll ask you to agree to some ground rules, and I will help you identify common ground, needs, and issues to be worked out. Our goal is an agreement everyone can live with. When we get that, we'll write up the agreement, have everyone sign it, and make copies for you all. First, the guidelines."

**Guidelines.** The mediator reads the guidelines listed in the table.

---

#### Recommended Guidelines for a Conflict Transformation Process

Everyone speaks in the first person, using "I" statements to express thoughts and feelings. Also, everyone speaks only for themselves and not someone else.

In most cases, participants speak to the mediator, not to any one particular person.

When each person is telling their story, there will be no interruptions. Listening is the key.

When sharing, group members stick to concrete observations and avoid generalizing, evaluating, or judging. If this guideline is not observed, the mediator will step in to "launder the language."

The mediation process and its contents are to remain confidential.

If anyone needs clarification on the process, they may ask.

(Add any other guidelines that seem pertinent to your problem.)

---

**Beginning well.** Take a few moments of silence for centering and grounding in God's love and light. Ask each person for a commitment to resolution and reconciliation.

**Storytelling.** Whether you are dealing with two people in conflict with one another or an issue in which people have taken sides, allow plenty of time for group members to share their point of view. This will take some time and requires patience.

• Each party explains the situation from their point of view.

• The mediator takes notes in order to summarize.

• The mediator recaps what has been heard and asks if everyone has understood each other's stories.

• The group takes a break so the mediator can organize for next steps.

**Problem solving.** The role of the mediator is to take information from the storytelling phase and identify three categories: areas of agreement, needs of the disputing sides, and problems or issues to be decided. The whole group then discusses what the mediator has identified. The mediator makes sure no one side or person is dominating the discussion.

The mediator goes over the problems listed one by one and asks the group to look for options for resolution on the individual issues. The mediator will encourage the group to emphasize specific, concrete solutions and refrain from giving opinions or judgments, encourage the group to work together to generate options, and paraphrase what they hear each side saying. The mediator should keep the focus on this question: "What can we agree upon today that will allow us to live in peace tomorrow?"

**When hurt feelings get in the way.** Sometimes the mediation process needs to be paused for a time of healing. This usually happens after someone has spoken harshly or failed to follow the guidelines by judging, evaluating, or otherwise moving from observation to critique. Begin with the compassionate-breathing exercise described earlier in this section. Then the mediator should restart the process as follows:

• Help the angry or hurting parties restate or launder their language, so that what they say has less potential to do harm.

• Ask the disputing parties to paraphrase to one another what they heard the other saying.

• Invite the parties to say something to the other (apology, statement of regret, amends, or perhaps a statement of appreciation for something) that might help them let go of their feelings.

• Ask for a statement of commitment to working together more peaceably in the future.

**Making an agreement.** The mediator has the group work out a concrete, specific agreement that spells out who does what, when, and where. The agreement should be balanced and free of bias, written out and then signed by all parties, and copied for all to keep on hand.

**Ending well.** Close the conflict transformation session with prayer, and celebrate the good work. Now you can get back to the rest of your work.

## EVALUATING PROGRESS

Several weeks or even months after action is complete, it's good to bring out the rearview mirror and look at how it all went. Consider the following questions:

- How did our awareness of God lead us to where we are today?

- How did our reflection on our life together contribute to our discernment?

- Did the action plan lead to the desired outcome?

- What were the high points of the discernment process?

- What were the low points of the discernment process?

- Now that we are beginning to see the fruit of our action, is there an aspect of this project that needs more discernment? (If so, apply the principles found in chapter 3 to the new discernment.)

- What part of the action plan was easiest to implement? Why?

- What part was hardest? Why?

- How shall we celebrate our journey from awareness to action?

We hope seeing the outcome of all your work using the Congregational Spiritual Road Map feels satisfying and inspirational. Taking that first step to act on our discernment takes faith. Hard work—done in community, bathed in prayer and spiritual sharing—can revitalize a church. You may want to mark the completion of the discerned action with a narrative description of the project written for the historical archives of your church.

Why not pause at this point to celebrate your work? Hopefully, those participating in this process are so excited and enthused about the outcome that others will want to be in on the next discernment-to-action project.

Even though you may have completed your work, the Spirit is always beckoning us forward, asking us to reflect on our action and its impact on the world. And that is what we will take up in depth in our final chapter.

# Action and Contemplation

Your ancient ruins shall be rebuilt;
    you shall raise up the foundations of many generations;
you shall be called the repairer of the breach,
    the restorer of streets to live in.
—Isaiah 58:12

A relevant criticism of contemplation and other spiritual practices is that focusing on spiritual practices can result in spiritual navel gazing. While spiritual practices are valuable because they draw us closer to God, some people worry that spiritual practitioners will spend a majority of their time in the interior life while matters of injustice are delayed or forgotten entirely. In fact, both of us have heard progressive Christians say that focusing too much on spiritual practices is a form of privilege that the poor and oppressed do not possess. From this perspective, the privileged have time to pray and meditate, while the poor suffer daily under the weight of oppression. We must pay attention to this critique, as well as to the injustices that plague our world.

An equally important critique, however, demands our awareness. Many people in social-justice circles observe that the work of social justice often does not feel grounded in spiritually based or contemplative practices. Such a grounding would root the justice work in a supportive spiritual structure, without which a group could easily find the work overwhelming or even potentially self-serving.

It is easy to feel outrage about the destruction of our planet, the gap between the wealthy and the poor, or the way immigrants are treated; it is natural to want to take action. Those of us who come from social-gospel and progressive mainline denominations or the peace church traditions feel called to stand on the side of the oppressed, as we should. While we (Chad and Teresa) agree that navel gazing will never create just social structures, we also believe social-justice movements that are continually resisting systems of oppression need to adopt spiritual practices such as discernment in order for practitioners to hear and receive clarity of where God might be leading them in the various activities of justice. Bruce Epperly writes in his book *Becoming Fire! Spiritual Practices for Global Christians*, "Self-care is at the heart of our domestic and political responsibilities, joining the inner and outer, and the contemplative and active journeys of mission and outreach."[1] Both are needed in order to hear or act along with God. Thus, the work of social justice begins within each of us.

As ordained clergy in the United Church of Christ, a well-known progressive denomination proudly working to build "a just world for all,"[2] we are aware of this need to integrate action and contemplation. Many activists in churches are on the front lines of issues that matter and for which our spiritual energy is desperately needed. We see many who are deeply invested in the work of environmental justice, calling for an end to the death penalty, practicing just peace principles or to end racism, and much more. In our experience, among the challenges of working in these areas are exhaustion and feeling overwhelmed. The great Trappist monk Thomas Merton has said of these experiences,

> There is a pervasive form of contemporary violence to which the idealist most easily succumbs: activism and overwork. To allow oneself to be carried away by a multitude of conflicting concerns, to surrender to too many demands, to commit oneself to too many projects, to want to help everyone in everything, is to succumb to violence. The frenzy of our activism neutralizes our work for peace. It destroys our own inner capacity for peace. It destroys the fruitfulness of our own work, because it kills the root of inner wisdom which makes for fruitful work.[3]

The injustices in our world present overwhelming challenges—powers and social forces that prevent justice from becoming reality. Those working to build justice in the world can develop feelings of despair, depression, anxiety, even isolation and loneliness. In our estimation, if we are to face these significant challenges through the "root of inner wisdom," we need a community of support and a spiritual foundation, both of which could easily be found in an experience such as spiritual direction.

While the tension between action and contemplation is ancient, in recent years it seems that many contemplatives have come to see the roots of social justice within us. Rooting social justice within us suggests that the interior life of the social advocate is as important as the outer proclamations of justice. Franciscan Richard Rohr formed an organization, the Center for Action and Contemplation, based on this assumption. One of the center's eight core principles is, "We need a contemplative mind in order to do compassionate action."[4] Rohr suggests in his writing that the work of social justice or compassionate action requires contemplation and a deep rootedness in the work of discernment. Such discernment is critical because the work of dismantling systems of injustice requires the work of love, and such love is uncovered through the practice of awareness, which stands as the foundation of discernment. Thomas Merton said of action and contemplation, "Action is the stream, and contemplation is the spring."[5] That is, contemplation is the place where action finds its origin.

Action and contemplation together offer us a framework for the work of social justice. If God is, in fact, interested in healing our planet and building a just world, for God's will to be done "on earth as it is in heaven" (Matt 6:10), then it is critical for spiritual pilgrims to incline our ear and listen for what God might be saying and calling us to do. Action and contemplation embrace many aspects of the church's mission such as our individual and congregational sense of call and the ways we worship, develop educational resources, and steward our resources, including the money and energy we expend for building a just world. Action and contemplation can work together to achieve a variety of goals, but this chapter focuses on how they help us carry out the work of social justice.

## THE CHURCH'S WORK OF SOCIAL JUSTICE

One of the ongoing challenges of social-justice work is that there is no shortage of issues to be addressed. The wide spectrum of justice issues can seem overwhelming. No church or individual can effectively address every justice issue at the same time. Addressing just one of these issues can be overwhelming, let alone all of them at the same time. This means that because our spiritual and emotional energy is not limitless, we must trust that others are taking up matters we deeply care about but do not feel called to work on. Examining a few of them, however, gives us a glimpse into the challenge of integrating action and contemplation.

## ENVIRONMENTAL JUSTICE

One justice issue that is particularly vexing in its scope is the care for the earth and the effects of climate change. Environmental justice is rooted in the belief that God has created a world whose parts, including human creatures, are interdependent and that God has called us to restore and to care for creation. From the impact of fossil fuels, waste management, and renewable energy to agricultural toxins and the destruction of rain forests, there is no shortage of challenges. Many churches are taking on recycling programs, as well as challenging congregants to engage in a home audit of their environmental footprint. Congregations placing solar panels on their buildings are a further example of efforts to care for the environment.

As useful as attempts to reduce our environmental footprint are, additional challenges easily overwhelm them. For example, existing laws and ongoing corporate lobbying keep systems of injustice in place. So congregations and individual Christians need to pay attention to the complexities of the social and political arenas and become advocates for change by joining those dialoguing in local, state, and national settings.

Author and environmental activist Jim Antal has said of the church and climate change, "One of the most important roles of the church is to take responsibility for what it has done individually and collectively."[6] The general minister and president for the United Church of Christ, John Dorhauer, has said, "If we do not solve the issue of climate change, it will resolve all other justice issues for us."[7] There is, therefore, a sense of urgency that requires the church's attention, repentance, and action.

Unfortunately, some people believe that the work of contemplation slows down environmental-justice work. While we need to be aware of anything that might distract from the goal of environmental justice, it is our contention that such justice work ought to be rooted in a strong contemplative and earth-centered spirituality. In our minds, there is no separation between our relationship with God and our relationship with the earth. So while contemplative practices or the work of discernment may take time, such work may also clarify where we should direct time, energy, and resources to build a more just and environmentally sustainable world.

## IMMIGRATION AND THE BORDERLANDS

In recent years, one of the most challenging areas of public debate in the United States has been immigration, particularly along our southern border. Our southern border has always posed challenges as politicians have sought to create policy around immigration, but in the wake of the North American Free Trade Agreement signed in the mid-1990s, the southern border has been the site of increasing inhumanity that deserves our attention. While reasonable people can disagree on the efficacy and necessity of a border wall, the rise in the funding of Immigration and Customs Enforcement (ICE) and the US Border Patrol, or the legal status of migrants attempting to cross the border, the recent humanitarian crisis of migrant deaths in the Sonoran Desert ought to raise significant concern among faith communities.

In southern Arizona in a town called Sahuarita, a congregation of the United Church of Christ is doing significant humanitarian border work and justice advocacy on behalf of asylum seekers. The Good Shepherd United Church of Christ, under the leadership of pastors Randy Mayer and Rebecca McElfresh, has developed several ministries to address this humanitarian crisis. They have worked ecumenically to develop a new migrant shelter across the border in Nogales, Mexico. A group called Green Valley Samaritans (Green Valley is a community south of Sahuarita) offers water, food, and blanket drops in the desert for migrants traveling through the rough terrain. A group travels into Tucson each week to bear witness to the work of the Operation Streamline court, which processes the legal cases of migrants. Finally, a group builds memorials of crosses in the locations where the remains of migrants are found in the desert so their lives and stories are not forgotten.

These remarkable ministries of justice, advocacy, and compassion require a dedicated volunteer corps and pastoral staff. One of the ongoing realities is that the work in the borderlands causes exhaustion and stress that are hard to address because the need is so great. Additionally, because the work can be so overwhelming and exposes deep cruelty, it is not uncommon for advocates to feel despair and depression. As inspiring as it is to see the work of humanitarians and advocates for the asylum seeker, the struggle takes significant courage and stamina.

We wrote this book to teach and encourage contemplative and discernment practices, especially listening for God within congregations. Not all churches discern social justice as a part of their mission, but for those that do, listening for God in the midst of their struggle for justice is critical because it can help clarify missions and priorities in the work God has given them. As we see in the work for environmental justice and in the borderlands, action without contemplation has the potential to create unsustainable and unhealthy attempts to advocate for justice. Bruce Epperly expresses well this need for healthy engagement: "Our spiritual stature comes from the compassionate quest for a world in which every person might experience happiness, abundance, and growth. In the quest for social healing, prayer and meditation are not optional; they awaken us to the unity of all creation and the intricate and dynamic fabric of relatedness from which every life emerges."[8]

For congregations with a passion for embodying the gospel through social justice, the outer action must be rooted in the inner life of Christians and their faith communities. Our relationship with the Holy requires both action and contemplation and begins within. First, we must discern where God's call for justice, both collectively and individually, meets our mission as God's church. Rooting such work in contemplation and listening for God can be restorative, offer us new vision for the church, help us focus on the heart of the work, and open doors to new and creative ways of overcoming the injustices in our midst. Congregations that are involved in any work to resist oppressive systems and stand against injustices will benefit from inclining their ear to discern with God. Their listening will make them aware, reflective, discerning communities that take action along with God, rather than communities that act on their own.

## CONGREGATIONAL SPIRITUAL ROAD MAP FOR SOCIAL JUSTICE

Congregations that work in the areas of social justice as a regular part of their communal life need spiritual practices that can ground them in their work. In this road map, we offer a few contemplative practices to help connect the social justice advocate to a spiritual framework through practices such as walking meditation and the loving-kindness meditation.

### WALKING MEDITATION

We hope through meditation to increase our sense of calm and awareness of the present moment, letting go of our passing thoughts through the breath and returning to the present. Meditation can be done while sitting or while walking. For sitting meditation, we sit in a chair, on a prayer cushion, or on the floor with arms resting on our legs. Eyes are either closed or softly gazing toward the floor. In walking meditation, not only are we in motion, but also our eyes are open and attentive to our surroundings.

Walking meditation can be done anywhere and at any time. You can walk on a sidewalk, in the woods, on trails, or even in your home. Another option is walking a labyrinth, a form of meditation that involves walking a specific path. The goal of walking meditation is to be fully present to a light walking on the earth, your surroundings, and the moment right in front of you. Famous Buddhist monk Thich Nhat Hanh has referred to this practice of walking meditation as "peace is every step."[9] Each step presents us with the opportunity to clear the mind of distraction and to attend to the moment in front of us. This brings us clarity of mind and is a peaceful way to restore the heart, mind, and body through times of feeling stressed and overwhelmed.

To describe the practice, let's assume you have discovered a lovely walking path that loops around a pond. The following steps will offer both you and the world the opportunity to heal.

Before beginning to walk the path in front of you, stand with your feet shoulder width apart, grounding yourself on the earth. Take three deep breaths to center yourself and welcome the journey ahead.

Take a moment to set an intention for your walk. You might dedicate the walk to migrant children, the earth, or peace in places of conflict. Or perhaps you have a relative who is ill and want to dedicate the walk to them. There is no right or wrong intention. Simply name what resonates with your soul in that moment.

Gently and slowly begin your walk, being aware of each foot hitting the ground as you walk.

Become aware of and notice your surroundings: the earth

beneath you, the pond's water, the birds in the trees, the shape of leaves and twigs, and the sounds that catch your attention. Also become aware of any passing thoughts that emerge through the chatter of your mind. Simply let them go, and return your mind to your breath and to your surroundings.

One form of walking meditation is to repeat a short prayer or mantra to accompany each breath in and out. Additionally, you might coordinate your breaths with a certain numbers of steps. For example, you might walk four steps on the in-breath, reciting the mantra "Be still," and walk four more steps on the out-breath, reciting the mantra "Know that I am God." Or perhaps on the in-breath you recite, "Breathing in, I breathe peace," and on the out-breath, you recite, "Breathing out, I share compassion."

When you return to the place where you began, stop and be still, breathing deeply in and out three more times. At the end of your breathing, thank God for the time together, and thank the earth for providing the ground under your feet.

## LOVING-KINDNESS MEDITATION

A key practice for people of faith with a passion for social justice is the loving-kindness meditation, a practice that offers both inward and outward healing and peace. It is a way to intentionally send love, compassion, peace, and divine energy out into the world, and this sending forth can dramatically change the meditator's relationship with the world. It changes such a relationship because it makes us aware of the "other," particularly their creation as beloved, sacred, and divine. It overcomes division and heals what is broken.

Here are some of the basic words of the mantra within the meditation:

May I/we/he/she/they/all be strong and healthy, peaceful and at ease.

May I/we/he/she/they/all be filled with loving-kindness and happiness.

The loving-kindness meditation is practiced in various ways, using a variety of wordings. But here is one suggestion for working through this meditation. This practice can be done sitting or standing, alone or as a group. We have also seen this practice done as a part of a walking meditation.

> Begin by placing both feet on the floor and taking a few deep breaths to center yourself. Leave all distractions outside the room, and become fully present to this moment.
>
> Recite the mantra above, using "I" as the focus on the meditation. Then spend a few moments in silence. Feel free to sing the mantra to close that part of the meditation.
>
> Repeat the same process, using first "we" and then "he," "she," and "they" in the mantra. Each time, imagine someone for whom you are grateful, and send that person this mantra. You may also imagine a person with whom you have significant conflict or from whom you have been alienated, and send them this mantra. You may want to name those persons specifically, rather than using "he" or "she," for example.
>
> The last meditation is the "all" offering of loving-kindness. The word *all* in the mantra refers to animals, plants, friends, enemies, the earth itself, the universe, and all matter and

energy—literally all that makes up the interconnected world we share. This movement from yourself toward all creation has the power to heal, transform, and even alter our perceptions of all that is around us.

End this meditation with silence and a few more deep breaths.

# Conclusion: Thoughts
# for the Road Ahead

This book is an invitation into a spiritual journey. Many Christians make this journey as individuals. But while it is critical that individuals experience the spiritual awakening we have spoken of in this book, we are primarily addressing such awakening in communities of faith—an awakening they will experience when they incline their ear toward God. More than ever, people yearn to journey with others. We believe responding to this yearning for a communal spiritual awakening is critical for this moment, when a worldwide COVID-19 pandemic has heightened our longing for community, reminding us of our spiritual nurture and that our lives are deeply intertwined.

During this pandemic, epidemiologists around the world have identified the need to mitigate the spread of the virus by what is called social distancing, or perhaps more accurately, physical distancing. The term refers to the need for people to remain in their homes or at a sizable distance from others, so as to not spread the virus to one another. No matter which term we use, however, Christians recognize that God made humanity for love, for touch, for relationship, and community. Through the use of technology, we have found ways to be the church, to be in relationship and community, and to be present to each other in suffering without actually being in the same room or embracing one another. The physical distancing has clearly caused emotional pain. People who are dying cannot embrace or be embraced by their loved ones or even be in the same room with them when they die. At funerals, family members at a graveside are unable to touch one another in their grief, and some funerals are being postponed entirely. During these weeks, perhaps months, when congregations cannot meet in person, we are experiencing in our apartness the truth that the church is a spiritual community and just how crucial our communal life is.

What we are seeing in this pandemic only further demonstrates to us the need for a book that explores communal spiritual awakening. One of the callings of the church is to transform lives, to stir us from a state of slumber into action. Spiritual awakening can occur as a result of circumstances beyond our control, or we can intentionally open ourselves to it. Indeed, this pandemic is beyond our control, yet it is offering us a window into the spiritual needs of those who long for church communities, who are inclining their ears to God. Our hope for congregational leaders is that you not wait for spiritual awakening to be thrust upon you but that you desire it with such intensity that you begin this journey unbidden. We urge you to incline your ear, open your eyes, listen to your body, and allow yourself to become vulnerable enough to feel the stirring of the Holy Spirit.

In the chapters of this book, we spelled out our understanding of listening for God, and now in concluding, we offer an image that we hope will be helpful. Imagine the church as an improvisational jazz ensemble. Jazz musicians rely on the sounds and cues of the other players in their ensemble, and it is only through listening to each other that they discover and create such incredible music. Jazz musicians are in a conversation with each other, all playing the same song, but each member of the ensemble contributes their instrument's particular voice to the whole. For each player's contribution to work, the player must listen to all the other parts. This is what spiritual awakening is like in the church: we listen to God as a community, which allows us to hear one another and participate in God's music. Through the spiritual work of listening to God—through awareness, reflection, discernment, and action—we together discover and create God's song for our community and our neighbors.

## ASSESSING THE JOURNEY

The Congregational Spiritual Road Map we have laid out in this book gives your congregation and you as an individual tangible ways to journey with God, to step closer to a God who in love continually seeks us out, and to understand who God has called us to be and how we are to love and serve our communities. Discovering your why and your mission requires listening for God. In these pages, we have invited you to join us in wondering just how different the church could be if we all learn to be aware, reflect on that awareness, embrace discernment, and take action in concert with God. It is our sense that by doing so, we will experience spiritual awakening that can transform the mission and identity of the church.

Living into such awakening means giving voice to what we are experiencing and evaluating whether we continue to be in concert with God. Evaluation in the world of Christian spirituality is tricky because our God is full of surprises. But we live in a world that looks for confirmation of what is holy. At the end of each chapter, we provided questions to help you evaluate how the process of inclining your ear to God is going. Seven questions can help us assess how spiritually awake we have become.

- Do we feel closer to God?
- Do we have a deeper understanding of our connection to God?

137

- Do we feel increasing freedom to be who we were created to be?

- How is the fruit of the Spirit (love, joy, peace, gentleness, goodness, faith, meekness, temperance; see Gal 5:22) evident in us as individuals and as a congregation?

- Did the action plan lead to the desired outcome?

- Is there an aspect of this project that needs more discernment?

- Has our deepening connection with God moved us to act on behalf of the vulnerable and oppressed in God's world?

It is easy to fall asleep in the spiritual life. While Jesus was in the Garden of Gethsemane the night he was betrayed, Peter and the other disciples fell asleep. Jesus had to awaken them to what was right in front of them. Even though they had journeyed with him for three years and Jesus had told them in the upper room that he would be betrayed, they still fell asleep.

Tools such as the Congregational Spiritual Road Map will help us stay awake, though, continually reminding us that the spiritual journey is a spiral that goes deeper, not a straight line to our destination. We will begin the journey again and again, using the wisdom gleaned from past awakenings as we continue to listen to God. As the Congregational Spiritual Road Map becomes embedded in the life of your congregation and your own personal spiritual journey, you will become more attuned to God's presence and begin to discern and act in a more organic or natural rhythm and relationship with God.

We believe constant awakening is an invitation to learn to be the church, even as the way we express and define ourselves as church continues to emerge and grow. Embrace the journey.

Listen deeply. Remain open to the transforming power of God's Spirit in your midst. Incline your ear, for the God who is still speaking awakens us to a new day.

### Prayer for the Road

Loving God,

Help us incline our ear to you.

We long for greater awareness of you.

We seek to reflect deeply on our life together and where we see you at work.

We ask that you lead us in discernment, so that we make choices in alignment with your desires.

Increase our faith and connection with you so that we may be the blessing you created us to be in the world. Amen.

# Recommended Resources

Abbott, Chad R. *Sacred Habits: The Rise of the Creative Clergy*. Aurora, CO: Davies Group Publishers, 2016. Abbott collects voices from across the mainline to discuss the ways creativity is shaping the landscape of pastoral ministry and therefore changing the future of the church.

Antal, Jim. *Climate Church, Climate World: How People of Faith Must Work for Change*. Lanham, MD: Rowman and Littlefield, 2018. Antal speaks directly to people of faith as they work to promote climate and environmental justice. This work is grounded in bridging both social-justice and spiritual or theological frameworks.

Bill, J. Brent. *Sacred Compass: The Way of Spiritual Discernment*. Brewster, MA: Paraclete, 2008. Bill sheds light on the history, the understanding, and the way of Quaker spiritual discernment, including "queries" in each chapter for discussion.

Bloom, Anthony. *Beginning to Pray*. New York: Paulist, 1970. This classic book on prayer by a late Orthodox bishop has guided spiritual seekers for years. It is an easy-to-read introduction to prayer as awareness of the holy.

Blythe, Teresa. *Fifty Ways to Pray: Practices from Many Traditions and Times*. Nashville: Abingdon, 2006. Blythe guides readers in spiritual practices, including instructions on how to lead groups in participating in such practices.

————. *Spiritual Direction 101: The Basics of Spiritual Guidance.* Berkeley: Apocryphile, 2018. Blythe offers spiritual leaders a helpful guide, including how-to information on spiritual awareness, reflection, and discernment.

Campbell, Peter, and Edwin McMahon. *Bio-spirituality: Focusing as a Way to Grow.* Chicago: Loyola Press, 1985. This book is about how to listen to the wisdom of the Spirit as it is conveyed in the human body.

Epperly, Bruce G. *Becoming Fire! Spiritual Practices for Global Christians.* Vestal, NY: Anamchara, 2016. Epperly focuses on the ways Christian spiritual practices intersect with those of other faith traditions, and he shapes a more global vision for how Christians can live their faith.

Farnham, Suzanne G., Joseph P. Gill, et al. *Listening Hearts: Discerning Call in Community.* Harrisburg, PA: Morehouse Publishing, 1991. This well-written classic book on discernment pulls in principles from both Quaker and Ignatian traditions to help congregations assist individuals in discernment.

Farnham, Suzanne G., Stephanie A. Hull, and R. Taylor McLean. *Grounded in God: Listening Hearts Discernment for Group Deliberations.* Harrisburg, PA: Morehouse Publishing, 1999. This follow-up to Farnham et al.'s *Listening Hearts* is written specifically for group discernment.

Liebert, Elizabeth. *The Way of Discernment: Spiritual Practices for Decision Making.* Louisville: Westminster John Knox, 2008. Liebert offers a feminist's rewrite and explanation of Ignatius of Loyola's teachings on Christian spiritual discernment.

————. *The Soul of Discernment: A Spiritual Practice for Communities and Institutions.* Louisville: Westminster John Knox, 2015. Liebert outlines how institutions can use a process called the Social Discernment Cycle to find God's desire for the institution's transformation.

Linn, Dennis, Sheila Fabricant Linn, and Matthew Linn. *Sleeping with Bread: Holding What Gives You Life.* New York: Paulist, 1995. The Linns offer a beautifully written book on the practice of the Ignatian Examen.

Loring, Patricia. *Spiritual Discernment: The Context and Goal of Clearness Committees.* Wallingford, PA: Pendle Hill, 1992. In this booklet, Loring gives an excellent description of how the Quaker process of clearness committee is used in discernment.

McDaniel, Jay B. *Of God and Pelicans: A Theology of Reverence for Life.* Louisville: Westminster John Knox, 1989. This classic text in process theology offers a window into a theological framework for grounding all of life in reverence and sacredness, highlighting the spiritual understanding that we are all connected.

McKinney, Mary Benet. *Sharing Wisdom: A Process for Group Decision Making.* Allen, TX: Thomas More, 1987. McKinney is one of the first spiritual directors to write about using discernment for group decision making.

Merton, Thomas. *Conjectures of a Guilty Bystander.* New York: Doubleday, 1989. A collection of Merton's writings on a variety of topics that relate to his day, including his thoughts on politics, race, character, and the hope of spirituality.

———. *No Man Is an Island.* New York: Harcourt, 2002. Merton weaves together essays that address the deep need among humanity for a spiritual foundation, particularly around defining values, human longing and fulfillment, and living a life of faith.

Nhat Hanh, Thich. *Peace Is Every Step: The Path of Mindfulness in Everyday Life.* New York: Bantam, 1992. This book provides an introduction into integrating the practice of mindfulness and meditation into the mundane and everyday realities of our lives.

Nouwen, Henri J. M. *The Way of the Heart: The Spirituality of the Desert Fathers and Mothers.* New York: Ballentine, 1981. *The Way of the Heart* is highly regarded as Nouwen's most basic small book on the spiritual life.

Parachin, Victor. *Eastern Wisdom for Western Minds.* Maryknoll, NY: Orbis, 2007. Parachin, a Disciples of Christ minister, offers an A-to-Z list of spiritual practices and prayers from Eastern religious traditions that many Christians find broadens their understanding of prayer.

Phillips, Susan S. *Candlelight: Illuminating the Art of Spiritual Direction.* Harrisburg, PA: Morehouse Publishing, 2008. Phillips explores the wisdom of the spiritual journey by grounding the work of spiritual direction in the soul stories of her directees.

Richardson, Ronald. *Creating a Healthier Church: Family Systems Theory, Leadership, and Congregational Life.* Minneapolis: Augsburg Fortress, 1996. A respected church consultant offers his view on the emotional and spiritual life of congregations.

Rock, David. *Your Brain at Work: Strategies for Overcoming Distraction, Regaining Focus, and Working Smarter All Day Long.* New York: HarperCollins, 1990. Designed for the business world, this book offers great wisdom into how the brain works and illustrates ways to open oneself to new insights through meditation.

Rosenberg, Marshall B. *Speak Peace in a World of Conflict: What You Say Next Will Change Your World.* Encinitas, CA: PuddleDancer, 2005. Rosenberg is the father of "nonviolent communication" and offers a way of relating and communicating that evokes agreement and peaceful coexistence among people and groups. This is an excellent resource for conflict resolution situations.

Van den Brink, Erik, and Frits Koster. *A Practical Guide to Mindfulness-Based Compassionate Living.* New York: Routledge, 2018. This handbook of mindfulness provides exercises useful for slowing down the nervous system and connecting with the Divine.

Vennard, Jane E. *A Praying Congregation: The Art of Teaching Spiritual Practice.* Lanham, MD: Rowman and Littlefield, 2005. Vennard's book is an excellent primer for people interested in teaching spiritual practices to congregations.

Walsh, Roger. *Essential Spirituality: The Seven Central Practices to Awaken Heart and Mind.* New York: John Wiley and Sons, 1999. Walsh offers descriptions of seven important spiritual practices without using explicitly religious language, making this book good for congregations full of seekers and "spiritual but not religious" people.

Wolff, Pierre. *Discernment: The Art of Choosing Well.* Ligouri, MO: Triumph, 1993. Widely considered one of the best books on the Ignatian method of discernment, this includes a chapter on how to use Ignatian concepts without using explicitly religious language.

Yaconelli. Mark. *Contemplative Youth Ministry: Practicing the Presence of Jesus.* Grand Rapids: Zondervan, 2006. Long-time youth minister and spiritual director Yaconelli writes for churches wanting to use spiritual formation processes for youth ministry. However, the processes he describes are useful in any ministry context.

# Notes

**FOREWORD**

1.  Thomas R. Kelly, "The Eternal Now and Social Concerns," in *A Testament of Devotion* (New York: Harper & Brothers, 1941), 84.

**INTRODUCTION**

1.  Susan S. Phillips, *Candlelight: Illuminating the Art of Spiritual Direction* (Harrisburg, PA: Morehouse Publishing, 2008), 10.

2.  See "In U.S., Decline of Christianity Continues at Rapid Pace," Pew Research Center, Religion & Public Life, October 17, 2019, https://tinyurl.com/u7lreo3.

3.  Jay B. McDaniel, *Of God and Pelicans: A Theology of Reverence for Life* (Louisville: Westminster John Knox, 1989), 23.

**CHAPTER 1: AWARENESS OF GOD**

1.  David Rock, *Your Brain at Work* (New York: HarperCollins, 1990), 93–98.

2. Owen Chadwick, *Western Asceticism* (Louisville: Westminster John Knox, 1958), 42.

3. Evelyn Underhill, *Practical Mysticism* (Boston: Dutton & Co., 1915), 7.

4. Carol Lee Flinders, *A Little Book of Women Mystics* (New York: HarperCollins, 1995), 44.

5. Flinders, *A Little Book of Women Mystics*, 45.

6. John L. Nickalls, ed., *The Journal of George Fox* (Philadelphia Yearly Meeting, 2005), 11.

7. Richard H. Schmidt, *God Seekers* (Grand Rapids: Eerdmans, 2008), 317–18.

8. Henri J. M. Nouwen, *The Way of the Heart* (New York: Ballentine, 1981), 37–39.

9. Rock, *Your Brain at Work*, 87–98.

10. Anthony Bloom, *Beginning to Pray* (New York: Paulist, 1970), 85–86.

## CHAPTER 2: SPIRITUAL REFLECTION

1. Baal Shem Tov, MSS 8214, D. Kelly Ogden lecture slides, L. Tom Perry Special Collections, Photograph Archives, 1130 Harold B. Lee Library, Brigham Young University, Provo, Utah, http://sc.lib.byu.edu/.

2. Elizabeth Liebert, *The Way of Discernment: Spiritual Practices for Decision Making* (Louisville: Westminster John Knox, 2008), 55.

3. John H. Mostyn, "Transforming Institutions: God's Call—a Director's Response," in *Tending the Holy: Spiritual Direction across Traditions,* ed. Norvene Vest (Harrisburg, PA: Morehouse, 2003), 153.

4. We also speak of "consolation prizes," or gifts given to people who tried but did not succeed in coming in first. This definition is not particularly useful in the context of spirituality.

5. There is a difference between desolation and depression. Clinical depression can certainly be described as desolation, but teachers of Ignatian spirituality make a distinction between the two. You can be in a period of desolation and still be a functioning, healthy person, while severe depression is incapacitating.

6. This is an adaptation of the examen from Dennis Linn, Sheila Fabricant Linn, and Matthew Linn, *Sleeping with Bread: Holding What Gives You Life* (New York: Paulist, 1995). This book is highly recommended to those wanting to learn more about the practice of the Ignatian Examen.

7. Eugene T. Gendlin, *Focusing* (New York: Bantam, 1982).

8. Bio-spirituality is a term coined by Peter Campbell and Edwin McMahon to describe the experience of spirituality in one's body. Yoga would be one example of bio-spirituality, and the technique of focusing is another. You can find a wealth of information about the focusing technique and bio-spirituality at McMahon's website (www.biospiritual.org) and at the Focusing Institute's website (www.focusing.org).

9. Peter Campbell and Edwin McMahon, *Bio-spirituality: Focusing as a Way to Grow* (Chicago: Loyola Press, 1985).

## CHAPTER 3: DISCERNMENT

1. Mary Benet McKinney, *Sharing Wisdom: A Process for Group Decision Making* (Allen, TX: Thomas More, 1987), 13.

2. Ignatius of Loyola, *Spiritual Exercises*, trans. George E. Ganss, in *Ignatius of Loyola: The Spiritual Exercises and Selected Works*, ed. George E. Ganss (New York: Paulist, 1991). The *Spiritual Exercises* were first published, in Spanish, in 1548. They can be found in several contemporary-language versions today and online at the Internet Sacred Text Archive, Evinity Publishing, https://tinyurl.com/r9mtqtg.

3. Elizabeth Liebert, *The Soul of Discernment* (Louisville: Westminster John Knox, 2015), 55.

4. Liebert, *The Soul of Discernment*, 3.

5. Robert Barclay, *Inner Life of the Religious Societies of the Commonwealth* (London: Hodder and Stoughton, 1877), 254.

6. Warning: If you choose to read Ignatius's original writings, you may find some of his examples explaining discernment of spirits disturbingly sexist. Keep in mind the cultural differences between the sixteenth and twenty-first centuries. We prefer to read one of the many contemporary adaptations that do not compare women to "the enemy," aka Satan! You can find a list of some of those in our bibliography.

7. This process was inspired by classroom lectures from Dr. Elizabeth Liebert that one of us (Teresa Blythe) experienced in 1997 at San Francisco Theological Seminary. For an elaborate treatment of an Ignatian

discernment process, check out Liebert's book *The Way of Discernment: Spiritual Practices for Decision Making* (Louisville: Westminster John Knox, 2008). Teresa is deeply grateful for Dr. Liebert's teaching and writings in her formation as a discernment coach.

8. When the discernment becomes uncomfortable or impatience sets in, some people may object to the process, calling it "too structured." The structure, however, provides boundaries that allow emotional safety for discerners and freedom for the Spirit to lead. We recommend acknowledging the discomfort and staying with the process.

9. Jim Manney, "An Ignatian Framework for Making a Decision," IgnatianSpirituality.com (Loyola Press), accessed February 5, 2020, https://tinyurl.com/rsyq57x.

10. Liebert, *The Way of Discernment,* 67–69.

11. Ignatius of Loyola, *Spiritual Exercises,* nos. 184–85.

12. Liebert, *The Soul of Discernment,* 157–58. Permission granted by Westminster John Knox Press to use this copyrighted appendix in the road map. The appendix also notes that Dr. Liebert previously published a version of this process in "Discernment for Our Times: A Practice with Postmodern Implications," *Studies in Spirituality* 18 (2008): 347–48.

13. "General Business Procedure," *Faith and Practice: The Book of Discipline of the Ohio Valley Yearly Meeting of the Religious Society of Friends* (Cincinnati: Ohio Valley Yearly Meeting, 2019), 26, http://quaker.org/legacy/ovym/pubs/FaithandPractice.pdf, accessed March 10, 2020.

14. "The Clearness Committee: A Way of Discernment," *Weavings: A Journal of the Christian Spiritual Life* (July–August 1988), 37–40.

15. Many spiritual directors are trained in facilitating clearness committee processes. You could also contact a local Friends Meeting for the name of someone willing to serve in that role.

16. Find it at the "About" page at the website of the Center for Courage and Renewal, https://www.couragerenewal.org.

17. Jan Hoffman, *Clearness Committees and Their Use in Personal Discernment* (Philadelphia: Twelfth Month, 1996), https://tinyurl.com/rqsb2n9, accessed March 10, 2020.

18. Patricia Loring, *Spiritual Discernment: The Context and Goal of Clearness Committees* (Wallingford, PA: Pendle Hill, 1992).

## CHAPTER 4: ACTION

1. One caveat: Some of your discernment deliberations may be too confidential to share. Make sure the group agrees on what to share and what not to share, and get verbal agreement on confidentiality before the end of each gathering.

2. More on this concept is included in the chapter "Is It God We Are Hearing?" from Suzanne G. Farnham, Joseph P. Gill, et al., *Listening Hearts: Discerning Call in Community* (Harrisburg, PA: Morehouse Publishing, 1991), 39–50.

3. Mark Yaconelli, *Contemplative Youth Ministry: Practicing the Presence of Jesus* (Grand Rapids: Zondervan, 2006), 147–56. The section on "Gathering a Covenant Community" is an excellent guide for calling and developing volunteers. Although Yaconelli's book is about youth ministry, the discernment stories and concepts are valuable for ministry with people of all ages.

4. Ronald W. Richardson, *Creating a Healthier Church: Family Systems Theory, Leadership, and Congregational Life* (Minneapolis: Augsburg Fortress, 1996), 51.

5. Roger Walsh, *Essential Spirituality: The Seven Central Practices to Awaken Heart and Mind* (New York: John Wiley and Sons, 1999), 85–86. The exercise is adapted from his section on exploring fear.

6. Marshall B. Rosenberg, *Speak Peace in a World of Conflict: What You Say Next Will Change Your World* (Encinitas, CA: PuddleDancer, 2005). Rosenberg's process for nonviolent communication can be found in this book as well as in some of his other books. The process takes learning and practice and is best understood through the use of Rosenberg's books.

7. Rosenberg, *Speak Peace in a World of Conflict*, 23–24.

8. Erik van den Brink and Frits Koster, *A Practical Guide to Mindfulness-Based Compassionate Living* (New York: Routledge, 2018), 86. The guide is filled with mindfulness practices, and purchase includes a link to downloadable audio recordings of select meditations.

9. "The Mediation Process: An Overview," *Mediation Skills Training Institute Manual* (Lombard, IL: Lombard Mennonite Peace Center, 2007), D-7. The Lombard

Mennonite Peace Center in Lombard, Illinois, has trained scores of people in congregational conflict transformation. The center has excellent resources to offer. You can find them at https://lmpeacecenter.org/.

## CHAPTER 5: ACTION AND CONTEMPLATION

1. Bruce G. Epperly, *Becoming Fire! Spiritual Practices for Global Christians* (Vestal, NY: Anamchara, 2016), 159.

2. "Purpose, Vision, and Mission," United Church of Christ, https://tinyurl.com/tnctcg5.

3. Thomas Merton, *No Man Is an Island* (New York: Harcourt, 2002), 70.

4. "The Eight Core Principles of the Center for Action and Contemplation," Center for Action and Contemplation, https://tinyurl.com/t2kl9nm.

5. Thomas Merton, *Conjectures of a Guilty Bystander* (New York: Doubleday, 1989), 86.

6. Jim Antal, *Climate Church, Climate World: How People of Faith Must Work for Change* (Lanham, MD: Rowman and Littlefield, 2018), 13.

7. John Dorhauer, text message to author.

8. Epperly, *Becoming Fire!*, 176.

9. Thich Nhat Hanh, *Peace Is Every Step: The Path of Mindfulness in Everyday Life* (New York: Bantam Books, 1992).